Quarterly Essay

Quarterly Essay is published four times a year by Black Inc., an imprint of Schwartz Media Pty Ltd. Publisher: Morry Schwartz.

ISBN 978-1-86395-602-4 ISSN 1832-0953

Subscriptions – 1 year (4 issues): $59 within Australia incl. GST. Outside Australia $89.
2 years (8 issues): $105 within Australia incl. GST. Outside Australia $165.

Payment may be made by Mastercard or Visa, or by cheque made out to Schwartz Media. Payment includes postage and handling.

To subscribe, fill out and post the subscription card or form inside this issue, or subscribe online:

www.quarterlyessay.com
subscribe@blackincbooks.com
Phone: 61 3 9486 0288

Correspondence should be addressed to:

The Editor, Quarterly Essay
37–39 Langridge Street
Collingwood VIC 3066 Australia
Phone: 61 3 9486 0288 / Fax: 61 3 9486 0244
Email: quarterlyessay@blackincbooks.com

Editor: Chris Feik. Management: Sophy Williams, Caitlin Yates. Publicity: Elisabeth Young. Design: Guy Mirabella. Assistant Editor/Production Coordinator: Nikola Lusk. Typesetting: Duncan Blachford.

Printed by Griffin Press, Australia. The paper used to produce this book comes from wood grown in sustainable forests.

UNFINISHED BUSINESS

Sex, freedom and misogyny

Anna Goldsworthy

In October 2012, late in a year of political bickering, two speeches were delivered in Canberra. The first occurred in Parliament House during Question Time, to a small audience of MPs, the press gallery, a handful of political junkies and tourists. A prime minister with her back to the wall came out swinging: "I will not be lectured about sexism and misogyny by this man."

This man was the leader of the Opposition, Tony Abbott, who had objected to a text message sent by the Speaker, Peter Slipper, to a male staffer: *Look at a bottle of mussel meat! Salty Cunts in brine!* It was a private text – a clumsy attempt, perhaps, at flirtation – but now on the public record as part of a sexual harassment allegation. Abbott was sufficiently outraged by the "vile, anatomically specific language" to move to have Slipper sacked.

How does a prime minister defend such a distinctive condiment? Labor had compiled material portraying Abbott as sexist, but Gillard had been loath to use it. Now her reservations fell away: "I will not be lectured by this man ... Not now, not ever." She listed Abbott's remarks and actions, and badged them with a word introduced by the Opposition: *misogyny*. She did not step back from generalisation – "Misogyny, sexism, every day from this leader of the Opposition ... that is all we have heard from him" – nor from the cheap shot – "the leader of the Opposition now looking at his watch because apparently a woman's spoken too long." The calculation was apparent, the practised use of rhetoric: I *was offended when* ... And the press gallery's verdict was unanimous.

Politics as usual. Fail.

At the same time, another speech was heard by a great many more people. Broadcast on YouTube, it transcended its context – the salted genitalia, the market tests, its own cunning – and became a more intimate piece of theatre. Devoid of backstory, the speech's calculation is less obvious; up close, you register the woman's genuine rage, the tremor in her voice. Around her, the barracking and heckling provide a Greek chorus of amplification. There are gasps of shock from Gillard's male Labor colleagues (those great defenders of female honour); loud tut-tuts from the Opposition. Abbott sits in silence, but as his half-smile gives way to grim forbearance, it is clear that he registers the speech's significance better than the press gallery.

This is the speech that was relayed around the world, and viewed more than two million times on YouTube. Mothers reported sitting down and sharing it with their daughters. Many of those cheering for Gillard had no knowledge of Abbott or his putative sexism. In this version of the speech, the territory being contested was not Labor versus the Coalition, nor Gillard versus Abbott, but Woman versus Misogyny. It was not quite I *had a dream*, but nor was it "essentially about herself," as the political correspondent Paul Kelly described it in the *Australian*.

Why such a disparity in reception? The press gallery placed the speech in a political context. On YouTube, against a wider cultural context, it reverberated differently. The former Coalition foreign minister Alexander Downer interpreted this context for the *Adelaide Advertiser*: "Don't today's MPs know what people say at barbecues, in the pub or when they're just out with their mates? Don't they know lots of people say bad things and it happens all the time?" On *Lateline*, Kevin Rudd claimed a similar folksy know-how: "I believe that the Australian public ... are more deeply concerned about the bread-and-butter, back-to-basics issues that confront families, [one of] which is, will I have a job?"

But it seemed that part of the Australian public *was* deeply concerned about this, hence the enormous response on social media. Gillard enjoyed a resurgence in the polls. Australians had not been listening, and now we were. Why has this been the most celebrated, most energised moment of Gillard's prime ministership?

"I have spent a bit of time thinking about that, because I was taken aback by the reaction," Gillard later told me. Her conclusion: "I think it gave the words to a lot of women's experiences."

On the surface, it looks like the best time ever to be a woman in this country. Girls perform more successfully at high school and dominate tertiary study. At the time of writing, we have a female prime minister, a female governor-general, a female deputy leader of the Opposition, a female deputy Speaker in parliament. The richest person in Australia is a woman. And yet mothers still felt the need to share this speech with their daughters. *I was offended when* ... Are these words their daughters will need?

There is a charmed zone for a girl, shortly before she is ambushed by puberty. At eleven or twelve, she is usually taller than her male peers, more articulate and more confident than she will be for years. She probably spends a lot of time in front of a screen, words and images flickering in her eyes. Facebook, SlutWalks, Lady Gaga, *Girls*, *Mad Men*, gonzo porn, *Twilight*, *Fifty Shades of Grey*. What messages are being broadcast to her, and what messages is she hearing? Are they going to make her bigger, or smaller?

Somewhere in that conglomeration of words and images, a woman wags a finger at a man. *I was offended when* ... The misogyny speech was, among other things, cultural critique, and it gave rise to further cultural critique. In consequence, it affirmed a great many things: the relevance of feminist debate; the importance of social media; but also – in this image-centric culture – the ongoing significance of words. And if a mother sits beside her daughter at that screen, trying to equip her with tools for life, a good place to begin might be with a lexicon.

WORDS

Misogyny

> Because if he wants to know what misogyny looks like in modern
> Australia, [Tony Abbott] doesn't need a motion in the House of
> Representatives, he needs a mirror. That's what he needs ... Misogyny,
> sexism, every day from this Leader of the Opposition.
>
> —Julia Gillard

How frequently we used the word in the days following the speech, as if
we had never heard it before. It is a sexier word, somehow, than sexism:
it feels good in the mouth, a little squelchy in the middle; it confers a
small distinction upon the speaker. Many of those reluctant to identify as
feminist gladly denounced misogyny. It was the new sexism. Prompted by
evolving usage, the editors of the *Macquarie Dictionary* expanded the definition of misogyny from "hatred of women" to incorporate "entrenched
prejudice against women."

It sounds good on paper, like even more reason to get angry. The only
problem is that it creates a vacuum in the language. If misogyny is simply
dressed-up sexism, what word do we reach for when we encounter the
genuine misogynist: the man (or woman) who loathes us for having a
vagina?

The publisher Louise Adler, in the *Age*, neatly delineated the two words:

> Let us be clear: sexism is the daily routine of belittling we have
> all endured – inequality around the boardroom table, the pat on
> the behind, the grope at the Christmas party, being talked over or
> through, that assumption you will make the tea. Misogyny is a
> deep fear and loathing, it is visceral and often expressed in gynae-
> cological terms. The distinctions are important because otherwise
> an important debate is muddied.

Misogyny's verbal expression usually takes three forms, whether delivered by internet troll, radio shock-jock, political strategist or playground bully. There is the unforgiving assessment of a woman's appearance, frequently involving the word *fat*; there are threats or acts of violence, sexual or otherwise; there is the reminder of the fundamental shame of her sex, of her *cunt*. All are designed to silence her. The misogynist presents a remarkably consistent platform: *Shut up you fat cunt*. Frequently it is appended with *or I will hurt you*.

Likening a vagina to foodstuffs is not necessarily misogyny: it can be poetry or indeed foreplay, though Slipper's text messages carry a note of disgust. A more clear-cut example was supplied by the 2Day FM presenter Kyle Sandilands in 2011. After a News Limited journalist, Alison Stephenson, criticised his low-rating television show, he described her on air as a "fat slag" (a reminder of the shame of her sex). Methodically, he ticked the remaining misogynist boxes: "Your hair's very '90s. And your blouse. You haven't got that much titty to be having that low-cut a blouse. Change your image, girl. Watch your mouth or I'll hunt you down."

How widespread is misogyny? In March 2013, Angela Shanahan opined in the *Australian* that "nobody in the real world thought misogyny was important. And no one thought it was real." Others consider it omnipresent. Germaine Greer famously declared in *The Female Eunuch* that "women have very little idea of how much men hate them." In *The Whole Woman* in 1999, she expanded upon this: "A few men hate all women all of the time, some men hate some women all of the time, and all men hate some women some of the time." This is a neat formulation, but when you turn it on its head it remains equally convincing: "A few women hate ..."

But does the current of hate flow more strongly in one direction than the other? Julia Gillard's prime ministership was a clarion call to misogynists everywhere. Anne Summers has documented much of this in her book *The Misogyny Factor*, quoting Gillard's parliamentary colleagues, the media, the Australian public, Facebook pages and memes, responses ranging from casual slurs about Gillard's "barrenness" to incitement to murder.

Writing for Fairfax in October 2012, Gerard Henderson acknowledged that "Gillard has experienced a degree of misogyny," but concluded that she "has suffered no greater abuse than that experienced by such predecessors as Fraser, Keating and Howard." More recently, he suggested that "if Julia Gillard's supporters really believe the Prime Minister's political discontents are due to prevailing misogyny in a contemporary patriarchal society, they are delusional."

Identifying misogyny as a problem is not the same as saying it is Gillard's only problem, as much as those who deny its importance would seek to muster their opponents into this position. Clearly, it is as reductive to dismiss any criticism of Gillard as misogynist as it is to reject her ability to lead because she is a woman. Is it possible that she may indeed be a flawed leader, who has additionally had to contend with misogyny?

An Essential Research study commissioned by *Crikey* found that 61 per cent of women perceived more criticism in the treatment of Julia Gillard than a male politician would receive, compared to 42 per cent of men. That 19 per cent represents the difference in frequencies – that Pythagorean comma – between male and female perception. Some might attribute that 19 per cent to "delusion." Others might say it explains why these words are still required: *I was offended when* ...

*

Can Tony Abbott fairly be described as a misogynist, on the evidence in Gillard's speech? References to the "housewives of Australia as they do the ironing" sound quaintly archaic, as if he has been watching too much *Mad Men*. If they are coupled with his previous reservations about female leadership – "What if men are by physiology or temperament more adapted to exercise authority or to issue command?" – a portrait of male supremacism emerges, alarming in a potential prime minister. But I am not sure even that has tipped over into misogyny. As Annabel Crabb has written, "Mr Abbott has been guilty of sexism, and at times extreme dopiness, with respect to women. But a deep and unswerving hatred of women, 'every day, and in every way'? It's not a case I'd prosecute."

Has Abbott been aware of misogyny in the community, and the political capital thereof? It would be difficult to miss it, particularly when delivering a speech in front of signs describing the prime minister as a "witch" and a "bitch." Has he sought to shut this conversation down, as when he famously took a stand against Pauline Hanson and her lunatic xenophobia? Is turning a blind eye to misogyny the same as being misogynist?

Neither side of politics has an impeccable record on this issue. Labor was still basking in the moral high ground last year when the backbencher Steve Gibbons tweeted that the deputy leader of the Opposition, Julie Bishop, was a "bimbo." You could sense the dismay within the ranks, the collective deflation of righteousness. The prime minister, according to her office, "made clear to Mr Gibbons that his remarks were offensive and he has rightly apologised." Similarly, there was a note of wishful thinking in Nicola Roxon's response to a dirt sheet circulating about a female candidate for the seat of Gellibrand: "We might expect this misogyny and sexism from our Liberal opponents, but surely it has no place within modern Labor?" Yet the greatest assault on Labor's anti-misogyny platform came from the prime minister herself, tweeting a happy snap of herself with Kyle Sandilands – he of the "fat slag" comments – dressed up as the Easter Bunny. Sandilands had endorsed Gillard on his radio show; this and the photo sat uneasily with her contentions that "I am always offended by sexism" and that "this kind of hypocrisy must not be tolerated."

So perhaps Gillard is not quite the champion we would like her to be, nor is Abbott quite the villain. We might imagine a more perfect version of her speech, in which she accused Abbott of sexism, identified the misogyny her prime ministership had unleashed, and criticised the Opposition for failing to take a clear stand against it. In cyberspace, the speech travelled better because it blurred these particulars.

But many of the speech's detractors took issue not only with the particulars. Many of them took issue with the existence of this conversation at all, for prosecuting a "gender war" they saw as irrelevant.

I don't see it that way. If perceptions of misogyny are a delusion, they are a powerful one, afflicting a sizeable portion of the population. And if they are not, perhaps we need to work at offering some translation of what words and images might mean across the gender divide. It seems that certain words vibrate differently for men and women, not least a word invoked frequently by the Opposition: *shame*.

Shame

Wherever you turn in feminism, Germaine Greer has been there first. Monica Dux and Zora Simic observed that, while writing their 2008 book *The Great Feminist Denial*, "we felt [Greer] was shadowing us. Or perhaps we were shadowing her." Greer has written eloquently about the fundamental shame attached to femaleness. Thirty years after *The Female Eunuch*, she claimed that "genuine femaleness remains grotesque to the point of obscenity." Shame – particularly bodily shame – is the raw material of misogyny. There are many words for women that sound like hate: *slut, hussy, bitch, cunt*. Each tethers the woman back to her body, to the dark secret of her vagina, that cultural locus of shame.

What is it about the female body that generates so much anxiety? Is it because we have designated the female body our prime sexual site – thereby engendering a curious double vision in the way women view their own bodies, as both objects and subjects of desire? Or is it because it billows up in pregnancy, confirming our beastliness, disproving our godliness? Camille Paglia has argued that "disgust is reason's proper response to the grossness of procreative nature." Or is the problem that we each owe a female body our existence, and the debt is too large to forgive?

Whatever the reason, female bodily shame is everywhere. Girls are equipped with it at puberty, if not before, as a type of secondary sexual characteristic. It is as implicit in the nun's habit as it is in the defiant smile of the Girl Gone Wild, flashing her incipient breasts. It informs every sartorial choice a woman makes, every decision about how much flesh to reveal; her attempts to conceal the "flaw" of her wide hips; her furtive purchase of tampons from the 7-Eleven; the absurd proportion of each day she allocates to feminine grooming, to that denial of hair and blood and perspiration, of female bodily reality. It is piped into her home via breakfast television, as Kochie urges her to breastfeed in a way that is "classy." The message is clear, and it is everywhere: shame is to be her daily companion. Until she escapes her body, she will not escape her shame.

The shame of original sin was the shame of a woman. The very physiology of shame is feminine: blushing, withdrawal. It prompts us to make ourselves smaller, through dieting or modesty of bearing. Shame underlines our compliance, our fixed grin, our need to please.

Shame is a powerful silencer. When we deviate from the script – when we raise our voices – we are shamed into silence. In April, the aged punk John Lydon enacted this on Channel Ten's *The Project*, after the presenter Carrie Bickmore asked him a question: "Hey, hey, hey. MISSUS. SHUT UP. Whoever you are, shut up. Now LISTEN, when a MAN is talking, do not interrupt." But there are other, more covert ways in which this silencing is enforced. In *Media Tarts: How the Australian Press Frames Female Politicians*, Julia Baird charted the particular moral and physical scrutiny our female politicians have been subject to, "dumped or discredited with an intensity that has surprised even the most experienced observers."

Inevitably, shame has been a keyword for members of the Opposition, as they have sought to impugn the legitimacy of the prime minister. The word garnered further resonance in September 2012, when the 2GB shock-jock Alan Jones suggested to a Young Liberals function at Sydney University that Julia Gillard's father had "died a few weeks ago of shame." It was a remark that elicited nervous laughter from the audience. The Young Liberals club tweeted the following morning: "Brilliant speech by Alan Jones last night. No wonder he's the nation's most influential broadcaster!"

The remark was also recorded by a News Limited journalist, and – like Gillard's misogyny speech – afforded a different reception in cyberspace. There was an outcry on social media, and calls for advertisers to boycott 2GB. Like Slipper with his foolhardy texting, Jones was a middle-aged casualty of technology. Social media – for better or for worse – is a democratic medium, and here it trumped the male autocracy of the shock-jock. In the absence of public figures calling for civility, it presented itself as an unlikely moral force. As Amanda Lohrey noted in the *Monthly*, "Jones, with his ageing demographic, was made to look like a wooden prop in a museum display of old media. Social media has pierced his seemingly invincible aura." Despite protests that he was being "cyber-bullied," Jones offered a public apology, couched in terms designed to minimise emasculation: "Can I just say that there are days when you just have to *man up* and say you got it wrong" (my italics).

Jones's remark was clearly reprehensible, but was it also misogynistic? Would he have made the same remark about the father of a male politician? Paternal shame at the wayward daughter is a loaded concept. Its darkest manifestation is the honour killing – although in Jones's formulation, Gillard's father visited this punishment upon himself. Closer to home, it speaks to the ancient disgrace of having a daughter on the stage: the shame of female visibility.

Tony Abbott claimed to have used the word shame in parliament at least seventeen times before the Jones incident. After such an outcry, you would imagine he might retire it from his vocabulary. And yet, less than two weeks later, he prosecuted the case for a motion against Slipper in the following terms: "Every day this Prime Minister stands in this Parliament to defend this Speaker will be another day of shame for this Parliament … which should already have *died of shame*."

Was there calculation behind this, an assessment that the political capital of this phrase was worth its price? Or was it just a verbal tic, the reflexive grab for the closest weapon to hand? Only Abbott knows. But by reaching for it, he handed Gillard the trump card of her misogyny speech, delivered with that magnificent tremor in her voice: "the government is not *dying of shame*, my father did not *die of shame*."

*

Some of us are equipped with this internal sounding board of shame; some of us are not. Perhaps this explains that Pythagorean comma: those harmonic differences in what we hear. Much of the material in Gillard's speech resonates loudly with shame:

> I was offended too by the sexism, by the misogyny of the Leader of the Opposition catcalling across this table at me as I sit here as Prime Minister – [she quotes him] "If the Prime Minister wants to, politically speaking, make an honest woman of herself ..." – something that would never have been said to any man sitting in this chair.

Although almost one in ten Australians lives in a de facto relationship, there are those who consider it to be living in sin. And in any sinful arrangement, the shame sticks more to the woman than to the man. It is to these people that Abbott directs the remark "honest woman," as a coded reminder of the prime minister's marital status. The expression "honest woman" thus serves a double purpose, as it reinforces Abbott's branding of Gillard as a liar.

> I was offended when the Leader of the Opposition went outside in the front of Parliament and stood next to a sign that said "Ditch the witch." I was offended when the Leader of the Opposition stood next to a sign that described me as a man's bitch.

Abbott did not make these signs himself, nor did he utter the words "bitch" or "witch." But when he delivered a speech in front of them, at an anti-carbon tax rally in 2011, it was inevitably taken as tacit endorsement. One sign said "Ditch the Witch," accompanied by an archetypal silhouette of a witch on a broomstick; the other said "Juliar ... Bob Brown's Bitch," with flames licking the words. Abbott later admitted that "I think a few people went over the top. Naturally, I regret that. But I can understand why people feel very passionate."

Lynch mobs are passionate. Crimes of passion are passionate. What else do these signs convey, beyond passion?

To begin with the language: *bitch* is a useful all-purpose term for the misogynist. It connotes a malicious woman, a lewd woman, or increasingly – a usage common in pop culture, particularly hip hop – any woman. Like other female insults, it can be repurposed to insult men by likening them to women. As a verb, it dismisses female complaint and female gossip. It also signifies sexual ownership, being mounted or dominated. This is a concept the blogger Larry Pickering has explored extensively in his visual representations of the Brown–Gillard relationship, and it is the meaning implied here, fuelled by sexual shame.

The *witch* is an atavistic concept, less overtly sexual than *bitch*, but also animated by sexual anxiety: of the unmarried woman, of female power and seduction and the casting of spells. It can also be used to denigrate a woman who has outgrown her sexual utility: the *crone* or the *harridan*, as the Liberal MP Christopher Pyne has described the prime minister. (Another of Pyne's – and Kevin Rudd's – monikers for the prime minister is "Lady Macbeth," the female embodiment of evil.)

The figure of the witch was invoked in Britain this year, as revellers flooded into the streets of Brixton to celebrate "Margaret Thatcher Death Day," bearing signs saying, "DING DONG THE WITCH IS DEAD." The words "Ding Dong" reverberated through Twitter; the song "Ding Dong the Witch is Dead" climbed the UK singles charts. The notion that we should not speak ill of the dead is a foolish one, yet there was something chilling about our cultural readiness to reach for this archetype. *Witch* has a currency that reaches deeper than political persuasion.

Traditionally, the witch would be hung or drowned or preferably burned to death, as this was considered the more painful mode of execution. The flames licking the words "Bob Brown's Bitch" flirt with this threat, lending the sign its charge.

Violence is the last resort of the disenfranchised man: if trumped by a woman, he can still fall back on brute strength. So perhaps it is not surprising that depictions of prime ministerial murder have arisen in oppositional discourse. In April 2012, the Liberal strategist Grahame

Morris suggested on *Sky News* that Australians "ought to be kicking [Julia Gillard] to death." Alan Jones has contributed much to this discussion, not least with his chaff bag conceit. In June 2011, he announced on radio that he would like to put Sydney's lord mayor, Clover Moore, "in the same chaff bag as Julia Gillard and throw them both out to sea." Clearly chuffed with the chaff bag, Jones assessed it "too clever by half" in conversation with Leigh Sales, and returned to it repeatedly on air, even proposing male candidates for it such as Bob Brown, Kevin Rudd and Barack Obama. During the same Young Liberals dinner at which Jones made his "died of shame" comment, a Woolworths executive donated a jacket made of a chaff bag for auction, which Jones bid on and won. It was a "rollicking" evening, Jones later reported.

The gender card

The *New Yorker*'s Amelia Lester and *Newsweek*'s Andrew Sullivan both suggested Obama could learn something from the misogyny speech; the feminist website *Jezebel* described Gillard as a "bad-ass motherfucker."

Alexander Downer remarked on *Sky News* that "I think it is disgraceful to go around calling people sexist and misogynist." His objection was not that it is disgraceful to *be* sexist or misogynist; nor that it is disgraceful to call people sexist and misogynist *inaccurately*; simply that it is disgraceful to use these words at all. Neil Mitchell, interviewing Kevin Rudd, found the words equally suspect: "Is it legitimate to be throwing around terms like misogynist and sexist as a form of abuse?"

It was a persistent strain of commentary: this conversation should not be allowed. In a column for the *Sydney Morning Herald* titled "Gillard reveals true nature in playing gender card," the journalist Paul Sheehan suggested that "after using the Minister for Innuendo and the Compromise-General to play the gender card, the mask has finally dropped away to reveal the driver of the politics of hate in Australia." Miranda Devine, in the *Sunday Telegraph*, offered intelligence from the "real world": "playing the gender card is the pathetic last refuge of incompetents and everyone in the real world knows it. It offends the Australian notion of the fair go."

From these howls of unfairness, it would seem that the gender card were some infallible trump, that producing it from the pocket would cause one's opponent to wither as in the presence of kryptonite. I am woman. Gotcha! Perhaps some women are able to deploy it so triumphantly, but the gender card is frequently used in reverse. Like nagging or bitching, playing the gender card becomes a useful silencing term, through which female grievance can be reduced to phatic noise. As Julia Baird pointed out, "what women have understood 'gender card' slurs to mean is that if they call out sexism, they will be stigmatised as weak, or whingers, and their careers will be damaged. This is what female bankers, lawyers, academics and professionals everywhere learnt: cop it and move on, despite the cost."

There are many factors besides the gender card that prompt women to "cop it and move on": a reluctance to identify as victims, thereby reinforcing perceptions of female weakness; the Australian veneration of stoicism, of getting on with it; and, if a woman is successful in a male domain, her pride in the toughness it took to get there. The Facebook executive Sheryl Sandberg has pointed out that "within traditional institutions, success has often been contingent upon a woman not speaking out but fitting in, or more colloquially, being 'one of the guys.'" But the gender card is implicated in all of these. A woman who complains of sexist treatment is a bad sport. It is not fair play, and so — according to Devine's formulation — nor is it fair dinkum.

In her inaugural speech to Emily's List, Julia Gillard described her female colleagues on both sides of politics as "tough women, resilient women. They are necessarily tough because politics is tough, and politics is tough because politics is important. It shouldn't be easy, and it's not. Not for the women — not for the blokes."

We have inherited an adversarial political system, but we have taken it to new levels of incivility. Abbott has been repeatedly described as the most successful Opposition leader in decades, largely because he has delivered on his promise to be "a junkyard dog savaging the other side." But as our politicians abuse each other, we also abuse our politicians. We have a collective need to despise our leaders, as if – as for Aztec sacrificial warriors – the privilege of office must come at the price of personal sacrifice.

Within parliament, a successful sledge is one that is both particular and recognisable, such as Keating's characterisation of Hewson's performance as being "like being flogged with a warm lettuce." A successful sledge homes in on a perceived area of weakness, including appearance: Kim Beazley and his girth; John "spot the eyebrows" Howard. But what message is being conveyed to our daughters when being *female* is the weakness, is the Achilles' heel? Because this is the form that sledges against Gillard have repeatedly taken: *Lady Macbeth, harridan, (dis-)honest woman, barren woman.* Keating's sledges, while vicious, were unlikely to spill out of parliament and implicate an entire gender. Describing Hewson as "a lizard on a rock – alive, but looking dead" may be cruel, but is unlikely to provoke a dismayed self-recognition in a young man, or discourage him from entering politics.

Those who accuse Gillard of deploying the gender card argue that she demands special treatment because she is a woman, with outdated expectations of chivalry. *If it's too hot, get out of the kitchen* runs the cliché: if a woman is too delicate for politics, she should not be there in the first place. Gillard, clearly, is not too delicate for this environment. The problem is that other women watching will stay out – not because of heat, but sexism. The health minister, Tanya Plibersek, acknowledges that "you don't get to be prime minister without suffering the slings and arrows occasionally and overcoming them, but the thing that disturbs me about it on occasion is I never want a young woman to look at the treatment that the prime minister receives, and think, I don't want to do that job, because if I'm going to be a target like that, I don't want to let myself in for it."

Getting on with it

Downer accuses Gillard of "whinging." He concedes that "some of the criticism is unfair and some of it may occasionally be sexist. But she's the

prime minister. She should rise above that. As Thatcher and Clark did."
Ironically, *rising above it* is what Gillard has forever done. In the absence of
a clear philosophical position, *getting on with it* appears to be her personal
credo. A keen student of the fate of her female predecessors, she described
the "Golden Girl vortex" to Julia Baird as that phenomenon whereby "the
media decide they're the next big thing, [and] the reporting quickly
changes from what they do to who they are."

That men should *do* and women should *be* remains a persistent bias of our
culture, even as it bears no resemblance to the actual division of labour.
As the British broadcaster and writer Caitlin Moran recalled of her thirteen-
year-old self, "I didn't worry about what I was going to *do*. What I *did*
worry about, and thought I should work hard at, was what I should *be*,
instead. I thought all my efforts should be concentrated on being fabulous,
rather than doing fabulous things."

Gillard's strategy has been to deflect any speculation about who she
is, almost to the point of self-effacement. Despite having more to explain
than the average prime minister – besides her gender, there is her pro-
fessed atheism; her childlessness; her de facto living arrangements – she
has not provided any reassuring narrative of self, any *Dreams of My Father*
user's manual. Instead, she just keeps on *doing* stuff, resilient as a Duracell
bunny: forging alliances, making deals, retracting promises, passing
legislation. She wears her action as a kind of armour; her survival strategy
is to remain a moving target.

Getting on with it speaks to a recognisable truth of female pragmatism.
Guy Rundle has suggested that men "like glory and bullshit," but, "Women
are different, like it or not. They remain the household budgeters, the
domestically oriented, and in that sense, the greater realists." And so we
recognise a version of our own lives in Gillard's constant action: ridden
with compromise, dousing fires on many fronts, *getting on with it.*

In many ways it is a useful credo. Besides repudiating gender stereotypes, it means stuff gets done. But it runs the risk of over-correction. In
her avoidance of "personality-based enquiry," Gillard has created a void

into which her opponents can hurl insults with impunity. (One of the traits of the witch is inscrutability.) In the absence of clear evidence to contradict them, they stick. Hence the surprising durability of the *Juliar* moniker: it became a handle by which we could explain her.

Perhaps we have backed Gillard into a corner. Misogyny and feminism each obscure the face behind her femaleness. There are those who will vote for Gillard because of the sheer fact of her anatomy, a qualification that trumps any policy. These are the most devout members of the sister-hood, the ones for whom, in the words of Greer, "to be feminist is to understand that before you are of any race, nationality, religion, party or family, you are a woman." And there are those for whom Gillard's gender is the only disqualification required.

Getting on with it might promise some escape, except that it becomes a further form of self-effacement. Gillard is right to reject a cycle "where the news becomes not what these professional women politicians do – do they ask good questions in Question Time? do they release a good policy? – but who they are." But it is also reasonable that we should seek to know our politicians, as our decision-making proxies. Leadership is not only about doing, but also about being: a symbol, an inspiration. Barack Obama's virtuosity lies in his handling of the (sometimes parallel) currents of rhetoric and pragmatism. Even Australians, sceptical as we are of American Messianic rhetoric, crave something more than *stuff getting done*. We want to believe in something, evinced by how readily so many of us embraced the heady promises of Kevin '07. The politicians the public rallies around – Obama, Hawke, even Rudd – are those with a strong enough sense of self to exude magnetism. Unfortunately for the female politician, our culture rewards female narcissism above female egotism. And charisma is not available to the egoless.

Ironically, all Gillard's "doing" may yet petrify into a type of "being." After the abortive March 2013 leadership challenge, Mark Kenny in the *Age* likened her to "the liquid-metal cyborg in the film *Terminator 2: Judgment Day*," for being "unstoppable," and wondered whether Labor might start "explicitly marketing Gillard as Churchillian in her toughness."

By nature, Gillard's is a leadership of compromise, dictated by a minority government and the identity crisis of modern Labor. But if ever a leader was required with the vision and charisma to define a party, it is now. Part of the power of the misogyny speech was that it marked the moment Gillard went off message, the moment that liquid-metal cyborg came to a standstill. For a moment, her relentless agency gave way to subjectivity. I *was offended when* ... With that tremor in her voice, she stopped being a blur of action and became a person.

There comes a point at which female stoicism becomes complicity. Mothers offered this speech to their daughters as a necessary template. Of *not* getting on with it. Of being offended. Could this – paradoxically – be the enduring *image* of Gillard's leadership?

THE LOOKING CONTEST: FOUR CAUTIONARY TALES

The politician

Q&A, broadcast on Monday nights, offers a parallel version of Question Time. Tony Jones presides over a panel of politicians and public figures, who nervously field questions from the studio audience and home viewers on the issues of the day. Accompanied by a live Twitter feed, the audience response provides some barometer of public feeling.

On 19 March last year Germaine Greer participated in a panel on "politics and porn in a post-feminist world." She offered a succinct assessment of the prime minister, invoking Gillard's own ethos of *getting things done*: "She's an administrator, she gets things done, she understands that she has to constantly get people on side, give people jobs to do, make sure that they do them. It's unglamorous, it's not star material, but it's what she's been doing."

At this point her commentary took a different turn: "What I want her to do is get rid of those bloody jackets! ... They don't fit. Every time she turns around, you've got that strange horizontal crease which means they're cut too narrow in the hips. You've got a big arse, Julia, just *get on with it!*" The audience roared with laughter; the camera cut to panellist Christa Hughes, mouth agape with delight. As Greer must have predicted, this last sentence became the sound bite. Any complexity in her argument was overridden by that gleeful Tourette's moment, the ever-dependable punchline: *She's got a big arse!*

And so the prime ministerial arse became fair game. Early the following week, Tony Abbott agreed that "Germaine Greer was right on that subject"; in a later edition of Q&A, the satirist Barry Humphries claimed to have "got it better" with the observation that "Julia would be interesting on a bike ... just get a mental picture of that." When Greer returned to Q&A in August, she conceded that it was an "unwise speech," but defended her position: "You don't understand how tough it is for little girls who think that to have a fat arse is to be dead, is to be finished. Women are fat-arsed creatures. Go right ahead, Julia. Wave that arse."

On the surface, this might be a sound point. It is still accepted that the cruellest insult a woman can receive is one that impugns her appearance: hence the silencing power of "fat" and "ugly." Tanya Plibersek remembers being rebuked while campaigning for having a "fat face": "I had no emotional response to it all – I just didn't care whether he thought I was fat or not – but I thought it was a really unusual criticism. I mean, if he talked to me about letting down my electorate, if he talked to me about a policy issue I cared about, it would have had much greater impact on me than an insult about how I looked."

The employment participation minister, Kate Ellis, makes a similar point about one of her own *Q&A* appearances: "[The respondents] were saying *and Kate Ellis sitting there with all her Botox and her hair extensions* and at that point I thought – they're actually just talking rubbish, but they're focusing on appearance because they think that's the thing that's going to hurt me the most. And that's what people do with women, they think we care."

Perhaps Greer's remark was offered in this spirit, as a prophylactic insult, proof that such things should not stick. And probably it did not stick much to Gillard, who has sustained much worse and just got on with it. But by making Gillard's butt the butt of the joke, Greer only reaffirmed its relevance. This was fat joke posing as cultural critique. Any little girl who imagined that "to have a fat arse is to be dead" would have found little reassurance in the laughter of that studio audience.

*

Although it was not mentioned in the misogyny speech, there has been a constant hum of chatter in the media about Gillard's appearance: her earlobes, bottom, cankles, shoes, jackets, haircuts and even her spectacles, which opened their own Twitter account in January. We have in fact seen considerably less of the prime ministerial body than the body of the leader of the Opposition, and yet there has been an anxiety to remind us of its existence. Some of this has been idle gossip; some has taken a darker hue. In internet memes, Gillard's head is photoshopped onto giant female nudes. It is misogyny's standard fare: *You have a female body, shame! Back in your box!* Then we no longer have to listen to you.

Such scrutiny is not limited to Australia. Hillary Clinton described it as the "significance of the insignificant," telling the writer Ayelet Waldman, in an article for *Marie Claire*, that "I no longer fight it. I no longer complain about it. It's just what you have to live with." The demands of grooming represent a significant temporal handicap for the prominent woman; more problematically, they divert attention from her message. Senator Penny Wong finds it "trivialising that people want to talk about what someone looks like or focus on that rather than on an issue which is actually important." According to a veteran reporter quoted in Waldman's article, "the story is never what [Clinton] said, as much as we want it to be. The story is always how she looked when she said it, or what she was doing when she said it." It is as if we were capable of processing only one type of sensory input at a time. The noise of a woman's appearance — *too low heels/too high heels/shiny nose/inappropriate cleavage/frumpy dress/bad hairstyle* — drowns out all other information, and becomes a type of silencing, regardless of intent.

Gillard sees this as a "critical mass issue," suggesting that "if you look around the world at other democracies and the number of women, if there's a first female leader or a couple of very prominent women, then it's got to be *appearance appearance appearance* and then when it gets to more routine it falls away, because it's not as intriguing anymore."

But does *appearance appearance appearance* ever fall away? Although women are very well represented in our community, they have not been released from this scrutiny. The point is made constantly: *a woman must strive to be attractive*. Some celebrities, for being professional beauties, might invite such criteria, but it extends to all women. She might be a Booker Prize-winning author, politician, scholar, miner or comedian, but let's cut to the important question: *what does she look like?*

As a woman, it is difficult to take a stand against this. Should you question it, the scrutiny turns — inevitably — to your own appearance. Could this be sour grapes? Are you a poor loser in the looking contest? Or is it a perverse form of narcissism? Is it — as Naomi Wolf, author of *The Beauty Myth*, was frequently accused of — an attempt to draw attention to your own good looks?

The problem is there are no real winners in the looking contest. Beauty might be a form of power, but it is a limited power, predicated upon the approving gaze. It contains a note of beseechment, however artfully concealed. And it is a power with a built-in redundancy.

"I just turned 29 so I probably don't have that many good years left in me," confessed Gwyneth Paltrow to the magazine NY Rock in 2001. In 2001, a UK study found that women start to feel invisible at forty-six. Our definition of female beauty is inextricably bound up with youth, so that even with the most expert interventions, it becomes an investment of ever-diminishing returns. According to this equation, the best one can hope for after a certain age is to be a fascinating freak, a youth impersonator: Joan Collins at seventy, Demi Moore at fifty.

For the beautiful woman, age is a particular cruelty. Perhaps there is a note of ambush in her expression: she is not practised in plainness, and age has caught her by surprise. Having escaped other laws of average, she imagined she might escape this too, that the usual rules of the flesh would not pertain. But age is a relentless democratiser. At some moment every woman realises the game is up: that she is now on the downward leg rather than the ever-promised ascent; that from here onward the Cinderella promise no longer applies; that she will not — *gasp* — be getting *any more beautiful*. And so her reluctant efforts in front of the mirror are no longer animated by hope, but by dutifulness, as proof that she has *not let herself go*.

It would be comforting to blame this on the patriarchy, except that women police beauty as much as men. We reinforce it as we comment idly upon the newsreader's hair, or as we pore — with moral indignation — over *Worst Dressed Celebs*. The journalist Natasha Hughes complained in the *Age* that you see "women in their lateish fifties ... schlepping about looking disgruntled with life and themselves. There's a bitterness, a resignation … I think it was Catherine Deneuve who said that getting ready takes so much longer as you get older. That the older you get, the earlier you have to get up to get ready just to look OK. She's French, of course, but why don't Australian women seem to do that?"

Perhaps Australian women have done the maths and found that getting up even earlier "just to look OK" no longer computes. Writing for the *Toronto Star*, the columnist Tracy Nesdoly found something to celebrate in this: "The wolf whistles may have stopped but, if I am to be honest, I'm grateful for the silence – there was a kind of invisibility associated with that as well."

It is futile to campaign against beauty. We are a visual species; sight remains our dominant sense. Women's and men's magazines alike are glossy tributes to female beauty. We are all looking, and we are all looking all the time. And beauty is beautiful. To do away with it would be to inhabit the bleak egalitarian universe of Kurt Vonnegut's *Harrison Bergeren*: "The year was 2081, and everybody was finally equal … Nobody was better looking than anybody else … All this equality was due to the 211th, 212th, and 213th Amendments to the Constitution, and to the unceasing vigilance of agents of the United States Handicapper General."

But if we are not to do away with beauty, could we at least reconsider its status as prerequisite? Not only to getting ravished, but to being heard? As a woman, you learn early that you are attractive or you are invisible. If you are invisible, you are frequently inaudible also. And so the young woman checks the eyes of the men she passes on the street, seeking a type of confirmation. To be desired is to be allowed to exist. Caitlin Moran has described fashion as a game, "but for women it's a compulsory game, like netball, and you can't get out of it by faking your period. I know – I have tried." But it is not only fashion that is compulsory: it is also hair and make-up and cankle-management and ensuring at all times that your bottom remains within acceptable limits.

"What kind of impact does this coverage have?" asks Julia Baird. "Well, firstly, it is a serious disincentive for other women to join politics."

The young woman glances away from Facebook for a moment, to join her parents to watch Q&A, for a brief window into adult discourse. What does she learn? That if she steps into the public sphere, she is asking to be undressed by the electorate. That if the prime ministerial arse is too big, it is quite possible that hers is too. That if she succeeds to the extent of becoming Australia's prime minister, she will still have failed at being a woman, because she's *got a big arse!*

The scholar

The early days of the internet promised some escape from this. With slow data speeds and limited bandwidth, the capacity for image dissemination was limited, and the net was primarily a text-based medium. Greer has found the printed text a source of oppression for women: "It is not until women learn to read that they internalize the masculine schema." But text offers opportunities too, for the reclamation of subjectivity; for invisibility without radio silence; for a holiday from the appraising gaze.

Like previous technological developments – from the car to the contraceptive pill – the internet offered further freedom from our bodies. It neutered the advantages of brute strength, rewarding traditional female qualities instead: verbal dexterity, relationship-building, "multi-tasking." To women isolated at home, it delivered social interaction and online employment. Mummy bloggers of the world, unite!

But other life-forms evolved in cyberspace alongside the mummy blogger. This proliferation of new life necessitated an apex predator – or perhaps an intestinal worm. In the real world, despite our disproportionate fears for our daughters, our sons are more likely to be victims of violence (overwhelmingly from other men). On the internet, it is different. A 2006 study from the University of Maryland found that a female username invites twenty-five times as many threatening or sexually explicit private messages as do male or gender-ambiguous usernames.

Why is cyber-abuse disproportionately misogynistic? Is it a reaction to the empowerment of women in cyberspace? Or is it an accurate reflection of what we are really thinking? Was it only our names that were keeping us honest?

Released from identity, we became all sorts of anonymous: *Anonymous* the vigilante superhero, anonymous the troll. We flashed our tits at Russian teenagers on Chatroulette; we partook of the darkest pornography; we pretended to be schoolgirls in order to seduce other middle-aged men pretending to be schoolgirls. Were we purging ourselves of our inner delinquents, or were we nurturing them?

Later we discovered this anonymity was imaginary: our screens had been watching us back all along. But we thought we had discovered a new mode of play. Everything was pretend, from our intimacies to our insults. We would not be held accountable, because our words were only virtual, not real.

Except that all words are both virtual and real.

*

Trolls, no doubt, are fascinatingly diverse creatures. Some abuse for recreational pleasure, reflexively – as when we hurl abuse at the television or at that moron turning right. Others have a clearer agenda: *pin the body on the woman*. She may have thought she had shrugged it off, out here in cyberspace, but she will not be allowed to escape so easily. In 2011, the feminist blogger Sady Doyle started the hashtag #mencallmethings on Twitter. It presents a familiar catalogue, a set of variations on that age-old refrain: *Shut up you fat cunt or I will hurt you*.

The truly obsessed troll, such as Gillard-obsessive Larry Pickering, or the anonymous tormentor of media personality Marieke Hardy, practises a trade that transcends silencing. This type of troll might establish an entire blog solely for the purposes of harassment, in which he lovingly doctors images of his obsession, picturing her in the nude, adding sex toys or accessories, just like his very own RealDoll (she does not answer back). Trolling of this kind becomes an inverted form of homage, the warped adult version of the inarticulate schoolboy crush. The boy tugs on the plaits of the girl sitting in front of him because she has disturbed him and the only response he can think of is to disturb her back.

How does the object of such fascination respond? The popular wisdom is, "Don't feed the trolls." But is not feeding the trolls just another version of *getting on with it?* Is this yet more stoicism as complicity?

*

The Cambridge classicist Mary Beard cuts a distinctive figure on television. With her long grey hair and make-up-free face, she violates the norms of female beauty. Last year, in his UK *Sunday Times* review of her BBC series *Meet the Romans*, the television critic A.A. Gill wrote that "Mary Beard really should be kept away from cameras altogether." Never mind that she might know something about the topic: she did not fulfil the basic feminine entry requirement of attractiveness, and therefore should not be heard. Gill maintains rigorous critical standards on hair colour, referring to his long-term girlfriend in reviews simply as "The Blonde"; when she experimented with brown hair, he pronounced her "shocking, common and twelve years older." Previously, he had reported of Mary Beard that she "coos over corpses' teeth without apparently noticing she is wearing them." On this occasion, Beard responded with a column in the *Daily Mail*, describing this as "a straight case of pandering to the blokeish culture that loves to decry clever women, especially ones who don't succumb to the masochism of Botox and have no interest in dyeing their hair."

Gill's rantings could perhaps be dismissed as those of a lone misogynist – or blonde supremacist – except that early this year, after Beard appeared on the UK television show *Question Time*, a small troll army emerged. Claiming to object to her remarks on immigration, her critics embarked upon an online campaign of harassment, until it became clear that it was not her views that they were objecting to, but the fact that she was expressing any views at all. Any argument Beard might have made could surely be trumped with female shame. And so the commentary focused on her long grey hair; on inferences about her pubic grooming; on speculation about the size of her vagina (an ongoing trope in Gillard vilification also), with photoshopped illustrations.

Beard claimed to be astonished by the "gobsmacking" misogyny. She elected not to *get on with it*, for the reason that it "would be quite enough to put many women off appearing in public, contributing to political debate, especially as all of this comes up on google." Instead she enacted her own version of *I was offended when*, reposting some of the most toxic material on her blog, part of the *Times Literary Supplement* online. In the fierce light of day, most of the trolls evaporated. The website that generated much of the worst content was closed down, and its moderator sent her an apology.

It was an unusual victory, not only against the internet troll, but also against the cultural objection to a woman of a certain age wishing to be heard. As if her presence in the public sphere was unseemly. As if it needed to be rebuffed like an inappropriate sexual advance.

The miner

In May last year, a panel was convened on *Q&A* with a showbiz bent, comprising Barry Humphries, the actresses Jacki Weaver and Miriam Margolyes, the journalist David Marr and the former politician John Hewson. The conversation meandered from foreign workers to the Craig Thomson affair to Charles Dickens. Early in the discussion, the subject was raised of Gina Rinehart, Australia's richest person. Barry Humphries proffered the hope that once she finished building a very big mine, "she can afford a hairdresser. Wouldn't that be wonderful?" Tony Jones cautioned the panel about "going down that path," but shortly a question was posed from Facebook: "Why is Gina Rinehart so greedy?"

As the producers must surely have anticipated, a collective assault upon Rinehart's character and appearance ensued. "Poor woman, she is not a beauty," mused Miriam Margolyes, "and I am not a beauty either so I know what it's like to be fat and ugly." Humphries' further contribution was, "I am not drawn to Gina. I mean, if I woke up in a motel with her on the next pillow I would ..." It was a reference to the legendary "coyote ugly" situation (needing to chew off one's own arm to avoid rousing an undesirable partner). Later in the same episode, he described the availability of satiric material as "never-ending. It's just like the hole; Gina's hole."

Rinehart contravenes our expectations of womanhood on several counts: by being ruthless in business and consequently the richest person in Australia; by seeming to be unmotherly; and by being physically unattractive. Her appearance lends support to her other failings: the moral equivalence of *letting yourself go* and bad mothering; the equation of fat with greed. This year, the Bald Archy satirical portrait prize was won by artist Warren Lane for *The Banquet of Gina and Ginia*, a portrait of Rinehart gorging herself on chocolate cake as her daughter watches.

Fellow obese billionaire Clive Palmer has also been an object of ridicule, but there is frequently a fondness in the reportage, locating him in the great Australian tradition of the larrikin. Rinehart is afforded no such pass. As was clear from the panel's discussion, our disapproval of Rinehart segues seamlessly into disgust. She may be a ruthless and unpleasant woman; she may have imperilled our sense of the impartiality of our press; she may provoke any number of legitimate political anxieties. But all of these are parsed into fat-hate. It was a weapon even used by her beloved father, when they became estranged over his relationship with his housekeeper, Rose Lacson: "Allow me to remember you as the neat, trim, capable, attractive young lady of the Wake Up Australia Tour, rather than the slothful, vindictive and devious baby elephant you have become … I am glad your mother cannot see you now."

Given the equation of flesh with female shame, more flesh can only amount to more shame. And so a woman eats less, to make herself a smaller target, to disappear her body, to conceal the evidence.

*

The morning after this episode of *Q&A*, the *Sydney Morning Herald* raved that "Barry Humphries' appearance on the ABC's *Q&A* program sent twittersphere [sic] abuzz last night – proving what most Australians already know, that he's one of the nation's greatest comedic talents." It was the highest rating episode of Q&A all year, averaging 816,000 viewers. On Twitter, #qanda trended nationally at number two and Barry Humphries at number four.

Consideration of the Twitter feed from the evening reveals the *Herald's* verdict was not unanimous. Alongside the celebration of the "CLASSIC double entrendre from Barry," "TOPICAL HUMOUR FROM OUR TREAS-URE BARRY HUMPHRIES" and "There's nothing like Gina's hole," there is also a sizeable contingent of dissenting voices: "Fuck, are we watching *Mad Men?*"; "Humphries ... use by date – expired," and – from Helen Razer – "all this 1972 dinner party is missing is a fish-bowl full of car keys. Disappointing, sexist antiques."

Comedy deals in stereotypes, and sexism remains a reliable stock-in-trade, afforded further charge today by the frisson of political incorrect-ness. We give our comedians licence, and they reward us by articulating those truths we might otherwise tiptoe around. But what truth is revealed through the "CLASSIC double entrendre" of "Gina's hole"? The unsavoury fact that she has a vagina? Why is this so funny?

Humphries' stock character Dame Edna could perhaps be described as misogynist; but then, in fairness, Les Patterson should also be described as misandrist. It is probably more accurate to say they are animated by a redundant version of Australian self-hatred. Geordie Williamson has observed the "dolorous truth" that "the world that Humphries had spent a lifetime directing his satiric genius towards was gone." As the template has fallen away – as our great-grandmothers have passed on, with their horn-rimmed glasses and Magic Silver White – Dame Edna has become less recognisable satire than independent entity. She has morphed from housewife to *housewife-superstar*, representing only herself, and offering Humphries the *maskenfreiheit* necessary for his particular – and virtuosic – comedy of cruelty. As Dame Edna loses cultural relevance, she perhaps attains a degree of retro chic; Humphries, in the context of this Q&A, looked eerily similar to her, as indicated by the tweets. Petrified into a national treasure, each of his utterances implied their own laugh track, whether funny or not. Perhaps Humphries has earned this reverence; he has certainly done his time. But without the large protective carapace of Dame Edna there was nowhere to hide the sexism; no satire in which to clothe it. Out of drag he seemed reduced, as unassuming as the Wizard of Oz, proffering schoolyard jokes about holes.

Among the blithe summations of a crowning night of television, there were dissenting views: the journalist Paul Murray, in the *West Australian*, described it as "vacuous crap"; the blogger Jeremy Sear, in *Crikey*, found it a "farce"; the former equal opportunity commissioner Moira Rayner, in *Eureka Street*, likened it to "the playground mobbing, the kind that ends with Piggy getting killed before the grownups break up the game of *Lord of the Flies*." Such reactions were only to be expected, according to Peter Craven in the *Sydney Morning Herald*, and therein lay the show's value: "The whole point of this Q&A was that it was potentially offensive to almost everyone and that's what made it such a revelation. It was likely to have legions of right and left-wing ideologues swooning with horror (as well as quite a few feminists)." He considered it "a wonder and a privilege to overhear," and "a fabulous odyssey of political incorrectness, of innuendoes and dreadful corny jokes, of great lunging lunacies and repartee."

Political correctness is an important term for the lexicon. Gaining popular currency in the 1990s, it was a necessary corrective to a rising cultural piousness. But like any cliché, the efficacy of *political correctness* has been worn down through overuse. Rather than carving out space for debate, it has increasingly been used to cancel it. By caricaturing any calls for civility as Stalinist brainwashing, it becomes – like the *gender card* – a useful silencing tool in its own right. It also contains a note of self-congratulation: of the user's own unfettered freedom of speech, her impeccable Australian credentials as a larrikin.

Watching this episode of Q&A, the *politically correct* viewer might note that Humphries could equally benefit from a good hairdresser, or at least a more convincing colourist. Perhaps she might also reflect that in the unlikely event of Humphries and Rinehart waking up alongside each other in a motel, two dismembered arms would be left on the pillows. But unlike Margolyes, Humphries did not consider this as he gleefully pitched his stones. This is because his house is not made of glass but of hide. It is reinforced with the genetic certainty that he will never be a contestant in the looking contest.

The novelist

Since 2010, the organisation VIDA: Women in Literary Arts has produced damning graphs illustrating the discrepancy between the number of reviews of books by women and men. These statistics have provoked a great deal of commentary, including the suggestion that women – by writing about "smaller" topics such as friendship, motherhood and domesticity – ghettoise themselves from a male readership. Similar criticisms have rarely been made of the male writer, lovingly documenting his midlife crisis. The assumption is that women, as the accommodating sex, are better prepared to read across gender. (This is an assumption borne out by the marketplace, as women continue to buy more books than men.)

Last year, Hilary Mantel won the Booker Prize for *Bring Up the Bodies*, the sequel to her Booker Prize-winning *Wolf Hall*. In these novels, she escapes any female ghetto into the brutal world of Tudor politics. The writer Sarah Waters observed to the *New Statesman* that "after a respectable but under-appreciated career of writing mainly about women, [Mantel] was finally recognised as a literary heavyweight once she produced a novel that was all about men."

In Australia in 2011, a group of eleven women writers, publishers, editors and booksellers established the Stella Prize, to celebrate the writing of Australian women. The first winner in 2013 was Carrie Tiffany, for her novel *Mateship with Birds*. In her acceptance speech, she said:

> To write – to take the work of reading and writing seriously – you
> must spend a great deal of time alone in a room. You must take

yourself away from being looked at, yet the pressure for women, young women particularly, to be constantly available for sexualised visual consumption – preened, styled, exercised, tanned, toxically enhanced – has never been greater. For women to spend time alone in a room, to look rather than be looked at, means rejecting some of this pressure. It means doing something with your mind rather than your body.

The only problem is that once the book is completed, the writer has to emerge from her room into the marketplace. In her 2003 memoir, *Giving Up the Ghost*, Mantel charted the physical effects of medication for a chronic medical condition: "Fat is not immoral. There is no link between your waistline and your ethics. But though you insist on this, in your own mind, everything tells you you're wrong." As a consequence, she braced herself for an inevitable strain of commentary following each book:

> One of my favourite grim sports, since I became a published writer and had people to interview me, has been to wait and see how the profiler will turn me out in print. With what adjective will they characterise the startlingly round woman on whose sofa they are lolling? "Apple-cheeked" is the sweetest. "Maternal" made me smile: well, almost.

This speculation reached a new pitch after Mantel's Booker victory. Lurking within every comment thread under each news story was the disapproving tut: yes, Mantel might be a great writer, but hang on – *she looks funny!*

Four months after her Booker victory, Mantel delivered a speech about the monarchy at the British Museum, in which she discussed Kate Middleton. Picked up by the British tabloid press, it became headline news. The speech, ironically, was largely about *looking*, about objectification – in this case, of the monarchy. In a striking passage, Mantel recalls staring at the Queen:

as a cannibal views his dinner, my gaze sharp enough to pick the meat off her bones ... and such was the hard power of my stare that Her Majesty turned and looked back at me, as if she had been jabbed in the shoulder ... for a moment she had turned back from a figure-head into the young woman she was, before monarchy froze her and made her a thing, a thing which only had meaning when it was exposed, a thing that existed only to be looked at.

Mantel deftly considered Kate Middleton in this context, "I saw Kate becoming a jointed doll on which certain rags are hung ... selected for her role of princess because she was irreproachable: as painfully thin as anyone could wish, without quirks, without oddities, without the risk of the emergence of character. She appears precision-made, machine-made."

In a culture which recycles princess scripts, it was a provocative line of enquiry. Perhaps for that reason the British tabloid press chose to misunderstand it, concentrating instead on manufacturing a catfight. The *Daily Mail* described it as "an astonishing and venomous attack"; even the *Guardian* found it to be "damning." Prime Minister David Cameron was prompted to announce that Mantel was "completely wrong"; Labour leader Ed Miliband pitched in, describing the remarks as "pretty offensive."

Mantel's words were indeed damning, but damning of a culture rather than an individual. Perhaps Greer intended the same with her "fat arse" comment – though unlike Greer, Mantel was not courting this type of attention. On the contrary, a nuanced speech in a museum unexpectedly became an event of national significance. Why should it have had such traction?

There was a certain punitive glee with which the remarks were seized upon: punishment, perhaps, for being a woman of a certain age, of a certain appearance, demanding to be heard. The front pages of the tabloids juxtaposed images of Hilary Mantel and the photogenic Kate Middleton; the reader was left to draw her own fairytale conclusions about princesses and jealous older women. Of course Mantel secretly wanted to be a princess – don't we all? – but had only become a Booker Prize-winning novelist.

It is a curious thing, our need to cast these eminent women as failures. (Howard Jacobson's inadequacy as a Calvin Klein model is seldom lamented.) Such scrutiny will not deflect Mantel's fierce gaze, but what is the young woman to make of it? *Images* versus *words* is writ large on her tabloid's front page. Which is more sexy? Which offers more power? Given such a context, the results of an Oxygen TV station poll should come as a pleasant surprise: only a quarter of young American women would prefer to win *America's Next Top Model* than a Nobel Prize.

Not everybody registering the novelist's apple cheeks is a misogynist. For many it is simply a reflexive sexism, experienced as category error rather than gynaecological loathing: *There is a fat woman in my newspaper!* as there might be *a fly in my soup!* It speaks to that fundamental knowledge: *women are primarily to be looked at.*

When did we learn this? I knew it already when I was six, and a *sexy legs* competition was declared during recess. And so the girls paraded in front of the boys sitting on the footbridge. I can still see my coltish legs, clad in brown ribbed tights and clumpy shoes, performing high kicks in the playground, seeking praise. Back then, I was not sure what *sexy legs* were, but I was sure I wanted them. It would not have occurred to me to turn the tables and judge those skinny legs on the footbridge, dangling from their short pants. But perhaps this is all that is required. We cannot stop them looking, or throwing stones. But we have eyes too, and can look right back.

And there are other weapons besides. It is no accident that the misogynist seeks to silence. Women are the verbal sex, which is why so many words have evolved to shut us up: *nag, bitch, gossip*. There is such power in saying. Beard's trolls scuttled away when she named them. Mantel commands something sturdier than *sexy legs*, and more enduring: words.

IMAGES

Facebook girl

For all our concerns about the new media, it does enforce a version of literacy. The young communicate through text more frequently than previous generations – SMS, email, Facebook posting and tweet, auto-corrected and predictively spelt, garnished with emoji or emoticons. Text remains critical to the workings of search engines, but optic cables and increased bandwidths have allowed the image to catch up. Facebook, YouTube and Instagram reign supreme. A technology that once offered some respite from the looking contest now leads us back directly to our own reflection.

The Facebook founder, Mark Zuckerberg, maintains that privacy is no longer a "social norm"; much of the media strives to make this true. All experience becomes performative, for an implied audience of Facebook friends or Twitter followers. It is more difficult to call in sick and go to the beach; it is more difficult to commit a crime and evade arrest; it is more difficult to do anything anonymously. Somebody will be there with their camera, ready to "tag" you.

Weddings have long been dominated by the photo shoot, staged less in the present than in service to some anticipated posterity: *we were happy then*. Increasingly, thanks to our smartphones, all of life is a photo shoot. In the 1991 Madonna documentary *Truth or Dare*, Warren Beatty bemoans the omnipresent camera: "There's nothing to say off-camera. Why would you say something if it's off-camera? What point is there existing?" We laughed, oblivious to the fact that within two decades this would apply to all of us. It is not only the tourist who needs to photograph everything to confirm it happened: we have each become tourists of our own living. Parties are photo shoots; brunch is a photo shoot; the kitty is a photo shoot. We rue the moment our child started to walk because we were not ready with the camera.

Perhaps there is something touching about this. It is an extension of the artistic impulse to memorialise: we have each become painstaking archivists of the moment. But there are some aspects of human experience that the internet does not cater for. It remains a virtual looking world rather than a virtual feeling world. Each time we post an Instagram photo – digitally altered to acquire an ersatz nostalgia – the question changes from *what did it feel like?* to *what did it look like?* Life is less to be lived than to be looked at. The danger is that repeated images of oneself *having fun* ultimately leach the fun out of existence.

For those of us who are "digital immigrants," in Mark Prensky's term, the technology retains the thrill of novelty. We still remember the non-airbrushed world we were born into. But what does it mean for our children to be "digital natives"? What does it mean for girls, trained already in objectification, to be raised on a Facebook diet?

Women are more active users of social media than men; they also use the technology differently. A York University study into Facebook usage found that "males displayed more self-promotional information" while "women displayed more self-promotional Main Photos." The study highlighted a tendency among narcissistic women to "include revealing, flashy, and adorned photos of their physical appearance," while narcissistic men preferred "descriptive self-promotion reflecting intelligence or wit."

The young woman is the celebrity at the centre of her Facebook universe, which might look like self-esteem but is ultimately a form of self-effacement. Because living for the photo shoot engenders a third-person experience. It surrenders the subjectivity of your own life, your ownership of I. By this, I do not mean the I of narcissism, which is in fact a refracted third person: "I'm the sort of person who … cries in movies/ is too caring/gives too much to my friends." (This is Generation Facebook's answer to the eternal adolescent question – *Who am I?* – couched in the vocabulary of the celebrity-in-waiting. The lines have been rehearsed for the *Big Brother* video auditions, or devised for the Facebook profile.) I mean instead that powerful I that exists not in relation to someone else's gaze, but claims its place as subject. An I that is not merely decorative; an I that forms relationships with verbs other than *to be*. An I that works or plays or desires or argues or makes jokes.

*

Facebook did not invent the objectification of women. There was always the beautiful girl in high school, expert curator of her own beauty. She moved through the schoolyard with her face slanted to the light, her best angles offered up to an imagined paparazzi. It was a face seldom disturbed by feeling, but arranged to stir feeling in another. When she became a model, she was coached in vacancy, and perfected the art of nothingness. Later she sought that same inscrutability through Botox.

Today's paparazzi are no longer imaginary. The girl's friends are her paparazzi and — thanks to the front-facing camera on her iPhone — she is her own paparazza. And so the young woman photographs herself repeatedly, both in and out of her clothes, striking the known poses of desire: the lips slightly parted, the "come hither" eyes, the arched back or cupped breast. She has rehearsed these postures since infanthood, schooled by popular culture. "It's like, I didn't ask to be born hot," says Chris Lilley's Ja'ime King. Perhaps she posts her "selfie" in an Instagram beauty contest, so that strangers can rate her beauty out of ten. Or she sends her naked image to a boy she likes, who shares it with his friends. Is it only by photographing herself that she knows she is real?

*

In their 2009 book *The Narcissism Epidemic*, Jean M. Twenge and W. Keith Campbell identified several factors contributing to narcissism in the millennial generation: reality television; indulgent parenting; celebrity worship; and the internet's promises of instant fame. They quoted the make-up marketing executive Samantha Skey: "we live in a culture of insta-celebrity. Our little girls now grow up thinking they need to be ready for their close-up, lest the paparazzi arrive."

This is great news for the make-up executive, but perhaps not such great news for the little girl. The very existence of make-up suggests a woman is not good enough, that each morning she must draw on a new face. She literally *makes herself up*, but it is a process governed less by creativity than by erasure. The language of make-up is that of concealment: *covering* blemishes, *correcting flaws*, *concealing* bags under the eyes. As she grows older, she has even more to hide: laughter and frown lines, evidence of *human being*.

The celebrity has an entourage to re-create her each day; the young woman must do it all herself. As the advent of machines did not liberate us from housework, so has technology failed to rescue us from our beauty regimes. The ubiquity of the blow-dryer created the expectation of perfectly maintained hair; now it is taken a step further, artfully arranged to look unarranged. WikiHow offers advice on *how to get tousled, sexy bed hair in eleven easy steps*.

To achieve the *Napoleon Perdis Nude Awakening* look, as seen on *Trinny & Susannah's Australian Makeover Mission*, all that is required is Auto Pilot Complex Skin Renewal Serum, Auto Pilot Pre-Foundation Primer, Sheer Genius Foundation, a Mighty Concealer Pen, Long Black Mascara, Color Disc Trench Coat, Blush Patrol, Eye Pencil in Onyx Factor, DéVine Goddess Lipstick in Electra and Luminous Lip Veil in In The Flesh. This will cost $427.50, and many hours of careful study; the happy result is that the woman will look as if she is wearing no make-up.

Rather like the most artful home-making, with its reassuring myth of a house that runs itself, so should the modern female bodily self-obsession conceal itself. Large quantities of time and effort are invested in looking effortless, in *sprezzatura*, in concealing the frantic doing behind all the being. The woman must tend her body, and then pretend to forget about it. *Oh, this old thing?* This *starved, coiffed, depilated, exfoliated, manicured, pedicured, exercised, moisturised, primed, plucked and painted old thing? It's just a little ... something I threw together.*

I am not sure that we can blame this entirely upon the "male gaze." Unless that gaze emanates from Napoleon Perdis ("not to prime is a crime"), it tends to register outline rather than detail, and is unlikely to detect skin primer. But there is no absence of other sources to prepare us for our close-ups.

There should be a word for the particular helplessness that descends upon a woman when she opens a glamour magazine. It would be something German and crunchy, a particular flavour of dismay. The details may differ from magazine to magazine – the heady cocktail of fashion and celebrity in *InStyle*; the high-church reverence of *Vogue*; the mandatory serious story in *Marie Claire*, consumed like homework before the reader earns the right to her narcissism – but they are all manuals of modern-day femininity. Each offers some version of *this season's must-haves*, of *ox-blood as the new black*, of *how to make key burlesque trends work for you*. Each promotes the view of life as a production, beginning with the costume department and make-up. The script can arrive later, if indeed it turns up at all.

Greer has suggested that "shopping is presented to women as recreation and they fall for the cheat." Even when we go looking for liberation, we find ourselves back at the mall. *Sex and the City* promised a reclamation of female sexuality and friendship, but segued into an infomercial for Manolo Blahniks. Presented as empowerment, it encouraged a generation of women to look no further than their shoes. (Carrie's reward for fabulousness was marrying Mr Big, who provided a closet large enough for the shoe collection. This presented an existential paradox: was the Manolo for the marriage, or the marriage for the Manolo?)

Of course it was always thus – chins were worn high in 1895, after all – but today fashion is more rigorously enforced than ever. Today's young woman has a much larger wardrobe than her predecessors, and on much faster rotation. She need not wait until next month's glamour magazine to discover her obsolescence: Twitter "speeds up the emergence of fashion trends," so that "no self-respecting fashionista is going to wait until next season's collections to see what's what."

Fashion can be an art form, if not the most lofty one. It can also be fun or frivolity or fantasy. But, as Caitlin Moran has noted, these pleasures are compulsory. There is no outfit a woman can choose that is ideologically transparent, devoid of subtext. Anything she wears comments upon sex in some way, upon its absence or – more likely – its presence. Perhaps she seeks to reclaim these messages, attempting Hipster Sexism: implied quotation marks around the *Mad Men* frock, or the stripper shoes, or the Playboy bunny on her T-shirt. This relies on the pre-emptive defence of irony: I *thought of it first*. But there are risks in being so knowing. Quotation marks are in the eye of the beholder. Late at night, when her vision becomes blurred, they might drop off altogether and she will find herself dressed simply as a stripper.

*

As clothing continues to disappear, the body itself becomes more stylised. The gowns of our forebears may have been restrictive, but they concealed any number of modern-day female sins: cellulite, varicose veins, leg hair, armpit hair, pubic hair. The more we were liberated from these garments, the fiercer the scrutiny we stepped into.

Female underarm hair started vanishing about 1915; leg hair many decades later. Pubic hair went missing more recently. We have thrown off the corsetry of our female predecessors, and replaced it with a corsetry of the body. Instead of buying a corset, we construct one ourselves through starvation, stomach crunches or plastic surgery. "Fat" is a keyword in the misogynist's vocabulary, but it is not only men who enforce skinny. (The women who grace the covers of men's magazines carry more flesh than those on women's magazines, albeit in improbable places.) It is also our high priestesses: those Devils who wear Prada, the magazine editors. Skinny women make better coat-hangers, and what higher female aspiration could there be than to be a coat-hanger?

Nudity itself has become so denuded that it no longer seems like nakedness. It is instead so elaborately stylised, so airbrushed, that it has become a sort of dress. Greer described the high-heeled shoe "as a marvellously contradictory item; it brings a woman to a man's height but makes sure that she cannot keep up with him." The current female bodily ideal takes these contradictions to a new level, as if assembled by a committee: a man's snake-like hips, the enlarged breasts of a lactating woman, a child's pudenda. This bizarre hybrid — like some mythological beast — is part earth mother, part ingénue, part beautiful boy.

One of the most radical things about Lena Dunham's hit HBO series *Girls* was the unapologetic way Dunham wielded her naked body on screen. The American shock-jock Howard Stern remarked on air that Dunham "keeps taking her clothes off and it kind of feels like a rape." Naked women are everywhere in our culture, so why should Stern feel so violated? It is because Dunham was not wearing her porn suit, but was truly naked: dimple-bellied, small-breasted, unapologetic.

Porn suits may be necessary when women venture out of the house more dishabille than ever. Perhaps they provide an armour when attempting the new gladiatorial sexual scripts, imported from porn (artificial breasts offering a measure of protection, like airbags). There are strict rules to this uniform. If a woman has pale skin, she must paint her body an Oompa-Loompa orange. Her teeth should glow in the dark. She should sport mermaid tresses on her head, but never betray the fact that bodily hair grows elsewhere.

In 1999, *Salon* magazine ran an article on a hip new Brazilian waxing practice. "You've changed my life!" gushed Gwyneth Paltrow, attributing a great deal of existential significance to pubic hair. The *Salon* author's friend Chad described his reaction to the waxed pubis of his girlfriend as "an unbelievably primal welling of emotion. First from the shock and then from the whole little girl eroticism of it."

Today, Chad is unlikely to be shocked. Bald is the new black (or the new oxblood). If he is under thirty, Chad is more likely to be shocked by the revelation that women actually grow pubic hair. Caitlin Moran finds much to lament in this, not least expenditure: "I can't believe we've got to a point where it's basically costing us *money* to have a fanny ... It's a stealth tax. Fanny VAT." She attributes the Brazilian wax's ubiquity to visual clarity in pornography, but surely there is more to it than that. As Chad articulates, it speaks to the "unbelievably primal" power of "little girl eroticism." By stripping a woman of sexual maturity, we also strip her of desire.

The actress Jennifer Love Hewitt has made several notable contributions to the female script, including, "I love to cook, so I can have a cake in the oven while I do a pole dance." In a 2010 appearance on *Lopez Tonight*, she introduced her own baroque interpretation of the pudenda: "after a break-up, a friend of mine Swarovski-crystalled my precious lady and it shined like a disco ball ... Women should 'vajazzle' their vajay-jays, I am currently vajazzled ... It's cute."

Perhaps a cute vajay-jay is an improvement on a vajay-jay that dare not speak its name. Indeed, it may be empowering to turn one's pubic region into a craft project: to reclaim it with sequins and glue. (How much nature can we take, after all?) There are other craft projects that involve more drastic tools. Prompted by the cute genitalia of pornography, labiaplasty and the quest for the "designer vagina" are also on the rise.

According to a study by the International Society of Aesthetic Plastic Surgeons, 15 million plastic surgery procedures were performed around the world in 2011. It is the logical outcome of female objectification: the woman buys herself a new body. Plastic-surgery tours to Thailand are becoming more popular among young women, promising that holiday promise of renewal, realised in the bra cup. Dr Bryan Mendelson, president of the International Society of Aesthetic Plastic Surgery, explained that his clients typically "have children and husbands and often a happy home life, but there is still something missing in their life and cosmetic surgery often helps them find that." What were they missing? Not God; not a meaningful vocation; not deeper human connections. They were missing a pair of silicone-gel implants, squelched through the inframammary fold onto their breast-tissue pectoralis interface.

Perhaps by acquiring her body through commerce rather than inheritance, a woman earns it more honestly. In *Not Your Mother's Rules: The New*

Secrets for Dating, Ellen Fein and Sherrie Schneider suggested that a

> woman with a nose that has a bulbous tip or a nose that is simply
> too wide or long for her face may need more than makeup. She
> might want to consider rhinoplasty ... We know this subject can
> be touchy with some women, but every client who took our
> advice and got her nose done is thrilled. It may just be an idea you
> consider.

In March, the *New York Daily News* reported that the latest nasal fashion is Kate Middleton. "I love the shape and size of Kate Middleton's nose and just knew I had to have it," explains Brianna Diaz, 26, an office manager. It is a familiar script. If you get the look right – if you sort out the costume – all will be well. The handsome prince will fall in love with your nose, and you will live happily ever after.

In October last year on *Q&A*, a young woman posed a question to the author and psychologist Pamela Stephenson:

> It's well known that you've undergone medical procedures to
> "modify" your body but people were created to age, so why defy
> the natural process of the human body? Instead of encouraging
> people to change who they are, shouldn't we be encouraging people
> to be happy with themselves and their appearance?

"The answer to the first question is *because I want to be a babe*," Stephenson replied. There was something striking about the way she said it, something defiant. It prompted a smattering of applause from the audience; a few co-panellists clapped, but they looked confused. Was this a *girl power* moment? What does it mean, anyway, to be a babe?

According to our conflicted, disassociated sexuality, *being a babe* not only means looking sexy but enjoying sex. Perhaps by acquiring an improbable pair of breasts a woman purchases a passport into the realm of the erotic. But what does the erotic now look like?

Porn star

Wandering home through a university college one afternoon, I get stuck behind a group of young men, handballing a football back and forth.

"What about the sandbox, when you fill up her pussy with sand!"

"The best one is the donkey punch, *uhuh uhuh uhuh*. Smash the back of the bitch's head when you're doin' it!"

I consider tapping them on the shoulder and reprimanding them: I *was offended when* ... But they are bigger than me, and there are more of them. Their voices are louder, equipped with the built-in megaphones of testosterone. And so they swagger through the manicured lawns of their entitlement, leaching misogyny into the afternoon air.

*

Imagine a world in which children's sex lives are being remotely programmed from Budapest or the San Fernando Valley. In the secrecy of their bedrooms, they are being fed very specific scripts. At first, they are repulsed as well as fascinated, but as they develop a taste for them, they are rewarded at their pleasure centres until they crave more, more, more.

Their scripts might not be our scripts, but how are we to know? Sexual performance, ideally, is one area in which we do not coach them. And so the usual generational structures of knowledge transmission do not apply. Sex is swotted from elsewhere: from peers, from magazines, from television, from movies. And today, increasingly, from online pornography.

My grandmother claimed to have learnt sex from a book. She suspected her mother never benefited from such instruction: "Even if she knew what an orgasm was, she would not have wanted one. It would have been just *too rude*."

We have come a long way since then, from the sexual stoicism of our female forebears. Women are no longer expected to lie back and think of England – or are they?

*

There is a liberal resistance to critiquing pornography. It sounds pro-censorship and anti-sex. Nobody wants that on their T-shirt. In his essay "The East is Blue," Salman Rushdie suggested that in conservative societies, pornography "sometimes becomes a kind of standard-bearer for freedom, even civilisation." By criticising pornography, you cast yourself not only as prude but also as supporter of the Taliban.

Some anti-pornography campaigners object to the fact of sexual intercourse, even off-camera. Andrea Dworkin famously described it as "a particular reality for women as an inferior class; and it has, in it, as part of it, violation of boundaries, taking over, occupation, destruction of privacy." But it is possible to support sex enthusiastically and still be troubled by the most popular pornography today.

This is because much of it takes the form of "gonzo porn," popularised by the porn actor and director John "Buttman" Stagliano in the 1990s. Pornography, as opposed to erotica, has always focused on the physical act, and in this sense gonzo is an uber-pornography. Featuring hand-held cameras and close-ups, it amounts to a renunciation of context, both visually and narratively. It feigns little interest in story but focuses exclusively upon mechanics, offering an instruction video of what goes where, even into the most unlikely places. The same mathematical question is repeatedly posed – one body, three orifices, how many appendages? – and repeatedly answered.

Gonzo pornography offers a very specific point of view. Here is the erect penis, in need of a home. There is the starlet, accommodating as a pin-cushion. Another phallus bobs into the frame, clamouring for attention. They line up in front of her, fleshy oversized lollipops, and she addresses her loving mouth to them. Yet more appear – will someone be left out? Resourcefully, she uncovers further orifices; she is nothing if not fair-minded.

Frequently, the starlet's ministrations are met with verbal or physical violence: strangulation, hitting, spitting. In a study for the journal *Violence against Women*, Ana Bridges and her colleagues analysed 304 scenes in popular pornographic videos and found that "88.2 per cent contained physical aggression, principally spanking, gagging, and slapping, while 48.7 per cent of scenes contained verbal aggression, primarily name-calling. Perpetrators of aggression were usually male, whereas targets of aggression were overwhelmingly female. Targets most often showed pleasure or responded neutrally to the aggression." As Cordelia Fine observed in her essay "The Porn Ultimatum," these figures represent forty-five times more violence than that identified in the 2008 Australian study *The Porn Report*, by Alan McKee, Katherine Albury and Catharine Lumby, in which similar acts are classified as "non-violent" because the recipient expresses no displeasure. Perhaps it is a relief that women's visible suffering should not be part of this script; or perhaps it is yet another way of stripping women of feeling.

In a 2001 interview with Martin Amis for the *Guardian*, Stagliano explained how he "evolved towards rougher stuff" with the Italian porn star Rocco Siffredi. "He started to spit on girls. A strong male-dominant thing, with women being pushed to their limit. It looks like violence, but it's not. I mean, pleasure and pain are the same thing, right? Rocco is driven by the market."

Is Rocco driven by the market, or is Rocco – along with his confrères – driving the market? Much of today's pornography is designed for shock alongside arousal, described by porn performer Nina Hartley as "*made-you-look!*" And as we become more open-minded, shock becomes a rarer commodity. "Shockvertising" is a form of advertising designed to cut through the clutter. The effect is yet more sexualised clutter: couples fornicate to sell sunglasses; women perform fellatio on ice-creams. Where then can pornography lie? The naked female ankle is no longer the thrill it was to our forefathers; her naked body is visible in every music video. All that remains is the secret of her insides. And so pornography reveals her splayed, turned inside out, distended upon multiple penises.

But surely there are other ways to be heard; why has misogyny become the attention-seeking technique of choice? On her MySpace page, the porn star Mika Tan observed that after almost ten years in the business, I have noticed trends toward more misogynistic roles. I think it is the change in American society's views on women. Women are more powerful than they have been over the last fifty years ... The stronger women get, the more men want to fantasize about them being put back in their place, so to speak.

In a 1997 *New Yorker* article, Susan Faludi interviewed the porn veteran Bill Margold: "We're the last bastion of masculinity. The one thing a woman cannot do is ejaculate in the face of her partner. We have that power." At the time, Margold feared the "masculine fibre" of pornography was imperilled by the "the feminization of Hollywood." What might masculine fibre look like? Faludi quoted the porn star and former boxer T.T. Boy: "I was a shy little kid when I started, and now I'm just a guy who wants to fuck the shit out of all of these girls. Just fuck 'em to death." Margold's fears proved unfounded: masculine fibre flourishes anew in the world of gonzo porn.

Gonzo offers a further type of revenge, upon beauty. Sexual power operates according to the rules of a scarcity economy, of being desired by more people than you desire. There is power in the way a beautiful woman collects the male gaze: *you can't have this.* (In this sense, the trophy wife is a roped-off area, an exclusive club with membership of one.) Sexual rejection disqualifies a woman from her femininity: the girl smiling bravely at the ball with her empty dance card; the spinster who was left on the shelf. But it also unmans a man. Many men, it seems, feel *bullied* by female beauty.

Several of the tropes of gonzo porn address themselves to this. The cum shot is a guarantor of authenticity for the literal-minded viewer: proof that his proxy has legitimately ejaculated, and was not just pretending. But when directed to face or breasts it also marks a type of possession, by defacement. As Margold explained to the psychologist Robert Stoller,

> my whole reason for being in this Industry is to satisfy the desire of the men in the world who basically don't much care for women and

want to see the men in my Industry getting even with the women they couldn't have when they were growing up ... so we come on a woman's face or somewhat brutalize her sexually: we're getting even for their lost dreams.

The porn star Ron Jeremy – fat, comic, hirsute Everyman – enacts a similar revenge, as an emblem of democratisation. The gangbang is further proof against exclusivity.

But why the overwhelming focus on anal sex? "Pussies are bullshit," Stagliano told Amis, and "what makes it in today's marketplace is reality." It is a line he repeats in conversation with the Australian researchers David Corlett and Maree Crabbe, as part of their new documentary *Love and Sex in an Age of Pornography*. Vaginal sex is easy to "fake," he explains, speaking admiringly of Siffredi for pushing women "a little bit harder in terms of doing a little bit stronger sex" until the "scene becomes something rough or something really interesting or real, and it's real because you can't fake pushing your limits sexually." To Stagliano, "the single most important thing gonzo has brought the world ... is reality."

But is the double penetration really reality? It is for some. In her lyrical memoir, *Affection*, Krissy Kneen described how:

> it is easy to disappear when there are two penises entering you. This is what I liked most about the double entry. As long as the smaller one is in the back there is barely any physical discomfort. It is easy to become a conduit, bringing the two men together, feeling them touch through the delicate internal membrane.

But there is a significant difference here to the "reality" advocated by Stagliano, in which the woman's discomfort offers a guarantor of authenticity. Although a passionate advocate for pornography, Kneen told me she finds "nasty and aggressive porn ... very problematic," because "people end up thinking all women enjoy aggressive sex," which "is not the norm and should not be presented as the norm."

Indeed, the porn performer Juelz Ventura suggested to Corlett and Crabbe that "people who do this at home probably have issues." Anthony Hardwood, a veteran of the industry, admitted that "some of the stuff we do is very over-the-top – you know you're not going to do this at home – it's just like crazy." He added, with some admiration, that sometimes, "you know the girl is very tough, because she takes everything." It is that celebration of female stoicism again. *She gets on with it.*

According to Corlett and Crabbe, these claims for reality are becoming self-perpetuating. In their paper "Eroticising Inequality: Technology, Pornography and Young People," they suggested that "porn has become a central mediator of young people's sexual understandings and experiences. Young people are exposed to porn at unprecedented rates. Many young people discover porn before they've encountered sex." They pointed out that pornography has a global annual profit of US$24.9 billion, and cited a 2006 study of thirteen- to sixteen-year-olds in Australian schools that found 93 per cent of males and 62 per cent of females had viewed pornography online.

This might be a relief to some parents: it spares everybody awkward conversations. But what does it mean to be part of a generation that has witnessed more sex than any in history?

Fewer surprises on the wedding night, for one thing. Having stared at numerous repetitions in close-up, today's teenager perhaps has a less mystical notion of the act. Divested of sentimentality, it becomes a physical activity, available to mastery. "That is where the market is taking us," wrote Amis, "towards heat, intensity, a frenzied athleticism." In Jonathan Franzen's novel *Freedom*, the rock musician Richard Katz laments the sexual professionalism of the young: "nowadays especially, the young chicks were hyperactive in their screwing, hurrying through every position known to the species, doing this that and the other, their kiddie snatches too unfragrant and closely shaved to even register as human body parts." Could this be modern love-making: hairless, virtuosic performance art?

Any performance ethic is only reinforced by the ubiquitous camera. Today's lovers not only watch more recorded sex, but also record more of their own. The thrill of exhibitionism should not be discounted – nor the career advantages of a sex tape on the curriculum vitae, as demonstrated by Paris Hilton and Kim Kardashian, among others. But by directing our pleasure to the camera, are we in danger of giving it away? In 1970, Masters and Johnson identified the sexual dysfunction of "spectatoring": of moving to a third person perspective during sex. Today, the third person is our constant companion, stalking us even into the bedroom.

Pornography imposes unrealistic expectations on both girls and boys: freakishly enlarged penises and breasts; a welcome mat before every orifice. "Every time I watch it I'd feel sad," a teenage boy confessed to Corlett and Crabbe. "I'm never going to get this chick, I'm never going to be this big." The same young man recalled his first sexual encounter, in which he "tried all this stuff and – yeah – turned out bad." Other young women are more accommodating. One teenager described how she tried to conceal the gagging reflex when being deep-throated, so as to protect the feelings of her penetrator. "When you love someone, you accept a 'pearl necklace,'" she shrugged. "It makes it a bit more exciting, when you can sort of think porn star. It makes it a bit more dirty, I would say, which is not a bad thing."

Of course she is right. Insisting that sex must always be a cosmic gateway to spiritual oneness, or that the heavens must part and rainbows appear, or that sex can only mean I love you is also restrictive. Sex can be many things. But it begins to look like one thing only, with porn agent Mark Spiegler estimating that gonzo porn now comprises 95 per cent of shoots.

It is not only tenderness that is erased from the gonzo template, but also, paradoxically, transgression. Under the forensic gaze of the pornographer, all is normalised; the sexual thrillseeker must look further afield. Greer described twentieth-century men as "like De Sade's jilted aristocrats, so sated with sexual imagery that they must behold ever more bizarre and extravagant displays before they can achieve potency."

Twenty-first-century man is yet more sated. A Padua University study found that a quarter of young men who habitually consumed pornography on the internet reported a fall in real interest alongside an increase in premature ejaculation. The researcher, Carlo Forester, concluded that "this new form of sexuality leads to isolation, a distancing from real sex and an alteration of sexual timeframes."

Hugh Hefner operates from the sexual script of a different generation, largely of his own making, and yet he offers a cautionary tale. There is a pathos to stories leaked from the Playboy mansion, of rigorously choreographed "sex nights" requiring a cocktail of medications, a queue of surgically enhanced bedmates on fast rotation, gay pornography on giant screens, and strenuous cheerleading from all parties. The octogenarian orgasm might sometimes require this sort of scaffolding, but it is so profoundly effortful that you have to wonder whether it is worth it. It is a commitment less to pleasure, perhaps, than to a notional virility. But it is also a story of hyper-stimulation, of a man who has been so sated as to have moved beyond the reach of arousal.

If pornography saps our young men of potency, what does it do to our young women? The problem with "pussy is bullshit" is that it means female desire is also bullshit. Stripped of g-spot and clitoris – two clear loci of sexual subjectivity – the woman is reduced further to object. Sex is something that is done unto her. The porn star Katie St Ives boasted to Corlett and Crabbe that "we're sexual athletes," and indeed the role requires great versatility and flexibility. But it remains passive, because her pleasure is not the point. Nobody is interested in her point of view.

The sexploitation films of the late Joe Sarno look a little quaint, not only because of the bellbottom pants and stilted dialogue ("Mama, I can tell you now … I'm a very hot, horny girl"), but also because of their archaic concern with female pleasure. Authenticity is registered in the pulse of a vein in a woman's forehead as she orgasms, rather than her guttural response to her sexual limits being pushed. And while they are frequently ludicrous, the sexual acts remain a two-way exchange (or three-way or four-way). They are a type of dance, not in a mechanistic, choreographic sense, but in the way the bodies interrelate with and accommodate each other.

When there is only one subject in a sexual act, it becomes a form of masturbation, regardless of the presence of a second party. And while the pleasures of self-pleasuring should not be dismissed, when it becomes the only option available, surely we are being robbed of something.

The second episode of Lena Dunham's *Girls* begins with a sex scene. "I knew when I found you, you wanted it this way," pants a young man.

"Found me where?" asks the young woman jiggling beneath him.

"In the street, walking alone. You were a junkie and you were only eleven, and you had your fucking Cabbage Patch lunchbox."

The young woman is Hannah, played by Dunham. She does not seem fully committed to her bedmate's fantasy, but she is a good sport, and makes the requisite noises. At the same time we register her puzzlement. She is trying to figure out how she belongs here.

SHAME AND SUBJECTIVITY

Desire

In Deborah Tolman's 2002 exploration of adolescent female sexuality, *Dilemmas of Desire*, she discussed the way we "parcel sexuality out, assuming that normal boys but not girls have 'raging hormones' – and that normal girls but not boys long for emotional connection and relationships." Desire, for Tolman, "is one form of knowledge, gained through the body: In desiring, I know that I exist." Its disavowal might not be the work of the misogynist, but the results are similar: a silencing, a relinquishment of subjectivity.

From Elizabeth Taylor to Madonna, popular culture has broadcast conflicting messages on female desire and desirability. Tolman pointed out that

> at the same time Christina Aguilera sings about "what a girl wants, what a girl needs," she presents herself as a sex symbol, consciously turning her body into a commodity, an object of admiration and desire for others, obscuring how or even whether her own desires figure in her willingness to do "whatever keeps me in your arms."

Modern-day icons such as Lady Gaga and Pink provide some redress. "Gaga is not there to be fucked," wrote Caitlin Moran. "The end point of her songs is not to excite desire in potential lovers but the thrill of examining her own feelings, then expressing them to her listeners, instead." Camille Paglia, less admiringly, found that "Gaga, for all her writhing and posturing, is asexual ... Is it the death of sex? Perhaps the symbolic status that sex had for a century has gone kaput; that blazing trajectory is over."

Pink described her song "Slut Like You" as a "very unsophisticated way as a feminist to take the power back." The song begins with a declaration: "I'm not a slut, I just love love." She explained to *Glamour* magazine that "I've always had an issue with [the idea that]: 'OK, we've both decided to do this. Why am I a slut and you're the player? You didn't get anything from me that I didn't get from you.'"

She is not the first to reclaim the word "slut." The first "SlutWalk" was held in Toronto, in April 2011, in response to a local police officer's suggestion that "women should avoid dressing like sluts" in order to remain safe; subsequently the walks became a global phenomenon. There is some haziness around the exact meaning of "slut," whether it refers to dressing provocatively or exercising sexual freedom. On their website, the organisers claim that

> We are tired of being oppressed by slut-shaming; of being judged
> by our sexuality and feeling unsafe as a result. Being in charge of
> our sexual lives should not mean that we are opening ourselves to
> an expectation of violence, regardless if we participate in sex for
> pleasure or work.

Social judgment of the "slut" is not only expressed by the rapist; it is also expressed, as Pink says, by the very existence of the word and the ongoing double standard it represents. SlutWalks bear a familial resemblance to Reclaim the Night Marches, which began in Belgium in the 1970s: *We demand the right to walk the streets at night, without the fear of rape*. The rapist is unlikely to be deterred by an appeal to human rights, even when chanted in chorus; the protest's function, rather, is consciousness-raising. Many agendas collide in such marches, but with the accoutrements of suspender belts and fish-net stockings, SlutWalks become a repudiation of female shame.

The year of the first SlutWalk, 2011, marked another signal event for female desire: the publication of E.L. James's erotic novel *Fifty Shades of Gray*. Beginning life as "fan fiction," the work was inspired by the young-adult *Twilight* series in which the virginal Bella Swan falls in love with the dangerous Edward Cullen. The troubled male lead is a familiar archetype, from Emily Brontë to Mills & Boon. In *Twilight*, Edward's complications take the form of being a vampire: not only is Bella's hymen at stake, but also her humanness. While the book is animated by desire, real sex remains notably absent, with its Mormon writer, Stephanie Meyer, maintaining that "I don't think teens need to read about gratuitous sex."

Twilight taps a rich vein of adolescent sexual anxiety. In *Fifty Shades of Grey*, James offered a more explicit interpretation of its danger. As the story became more lurid, she removed it from fan-fiction sites to her own website, subsequently marketing it through the Australian ebook publisher *The Writer's Coffee Shop*. The book's original incarnation as an ebook partly explains its popularity. Women were able to purchase it anonymously and consume it on ereaders, without a book cover advertising its contents. As the ebook became popular, it garnered a type of legitimacy, and was eventually picked up by Vintage. It subsequently sold more than 60 million copies worldwide, retaining the number one position on *USA Today*'s bestselling books list for a record-breaking twenty weeks. The book is now read – shame-free – in public spaces from aeroplanes to cafes. This is a book designed to arouse, read by women who wish to be aroused, consumed with a level of public acceptance that even *Playboy* has not achieved. Technology thus offered a private incubator for female desire, until it was robust enough to step into the public sphere.

From a feminist perspective, all of this looks positive: the war on shame has many fronts. The book's content is more difficult to parse. Owing to its overwhelming popularity, it offers a type of census on female desire today – which in fact looks strikingly similar to female desire yesterday, only with edgier accessories. The 21-year-old virginal college student Anastasia Steele falls in love with the devastatingly handsome, wealthy and troubled alpha-male Christian Grey, who deflowers her. The book's central tussle is between two possible versions of a relationship – the romantic and the physical – with each protagonist tempted by the other's version. As the psychologist Leon Seltzer pointed out, the "ending of the romantic adventure is that whereas the innocent, submissive heroine may earlier have been sexually deflowered by the alpha hero, now he's *emotionally deflowered* by her."

This power struggle is complicated further by Christian's predilection for BDSM (bondage and discipline, domination and submission, sadism, masochism). The BDSM of *Fifty Shades* is far tamer than that of *The Story of O*, and worlds away from any Sadean precedent. Little takes place in the Red Room of Pain beyond spanking and mild bondage; in one PG-rated moment, Anastasia wears Christian's underpants, to the titillation of both parties. BDSM here is more significant for what it represents. Because it is not Anastasia's fantasy, her arousal can be shame-free. Tolman describes "it just happened" as a "cover story" for adolescent girls, "that covers over active choice, agency, and responsibility, which serves to 'disappear' desire, in the telling and in the living."

This cover story is not limited to adolescent girls. In her 1973 compendium of sexual fantasies, *My Secret Garden*, Nancy Friday suggested that despite growing sexual empowerment, a woman's

> fantasy will often still be of the "it is not my fault, he made me do it" type: She was doped, or raped, or subjected to cruel and over-whelming domination. Ideas like these, so deeply rooted in the mind no matter what the relatively free body does, will take another generation to outgrow.

Forty years later, we are yet to outgrow them. When desire is verboten, sexual passivity remains a necessary defence mechanism. Desire can only be admitted to under very particular circumstances. This is the significance of *Fifty Shades*. Through a complex set of circumstances (its genesis as ebook) women are able shamelessly to read about a woman shamelessly participating in sexual play ("it just happened").

Fifty Shades broadcasts conflicting messages on sexual subjectivity. While it subscribes to the ancient template of female passivity and male sexual orchestration, it also maps Anastasia's discovery of her desire. Compared to the pincushion starlet of gonzo, she is anything but an object. For one thing, we take her viewpoint: "I'm squirming with a needy, achy ... discomfort. I don't understand this reaction. *Hmmm ... Desire*. This is desire. This is what it feels like." This is a book written by a woman for women. Words – however badly written – offer a better defence against objectification than images.

Like any self-respecting romantic heroine, Anastasia is *sassy*, prone to eye-rolling and smart comebacks. While this might implicitly be a posture of the weak, it offers more empowerment than the gonzo starlet's stoicism. More significantly, Christian remains as attentive to Anastasia's pleasure as he is to his own. Like Edward Cullen, Christian is empathetic to the point of telepathy. His unfailing command of Anastasia's orgasm might amount to another form of conquest, but at least that orgasm is the point of this book. Anastasia's pussy is not bullshit.

What is the feminist to make of this? Perhaps as a diversionary tactic, many reviewers have focused on the book's negligible literary qualities, when literature was never really the point. Taking a different tack, Katie Roiphe in *Newsweek* suggested that it

> may be that power is not always that comfortable, even for those of us who grew up in it; it may be that equality is something we want only sometimes and in some places and in some arenas; it may be that power and all of its imperatives can be boring.

There is an echo here of the porn star Mika Tan's theory about misogyny in pornography; the uncomfortable suggestion that men and women alike crave some corrective to women's advancement.

On his HLN cable show, Drew Pinsky labelled *Fifty Shades* a "rape fantasy," but much of the book is devoted to the issue of consent, to the extent that a contract is prepared. If anything, *Fifty Shades* offers a fetishisation of the idea of consent. Anastasia is courted not only for her maidenhead, but for her signature: will she or won't she sign the contract?

Dominatrices attest to the popularity of their services among "alpha males," for whom their services offer a relief from decision-making, described by Seltzer as an "alpha holiday." Could *Fifty Shades* represent this "alpha holiday," in this case for an entire gender?

Or is it possible that this book does not speak to a contemporary script at all, but to a more ancient struggle? Camille Paglia suggested that "in every orgasm there is domination or surrender"; this book, finally, is about the transmission of power, which would have little interest if the protagonists were not evenly matched. Christian might own fleets of helicopters and run a tremendously important yet entirely mysterious international business, but Anastasia can disarm him simply by biting her lip. When sexual power is the greatest power available to women, it is unsurprising they should fantasise about having more.

Doubtless there is more worthy erotica; certainly there is better erotica. But paths to arousal remain stubbornly resistant to both politics and aesthetics. Desire, at least, is a form of subjectivity. Is it feminist to tell women their arousal is not good enough?

Humour

Lena Dunham's *Girls* offers a different type of subjectivity. In season two, Hannah exchanges T-shirts with a stranger in a nightclub, pulling a yellow mesh tank top over her naked torso. "I usually hate when you wear your nipples out in public like that," says her gay room-mate, Elijah, "but you look so beautiful, Hannah." Hannah's nipples remain out for the remainder of the episode. Nosing from the mesh, they are far from ornamental, registering instead as an irritant. They add nothing to the drama beyond a low hum of corporeality, an insistence of sexuality over sexiness, a reclamation of shame.

The misogynist has limited power over Dunham. He could photo-shop her head onto a naked body – or he could save himself the bother and take a screenshot from any episode. Dunham explained to Emily Nussbaum that her nudity is partly inspired by the need "to feel some kind of ownership of your own body, the way getting tattoos does." But it is also a provocation: "Not 'Fuck you,' but a way of saying, with these bodies, you know: Don't silence them." She blasphemed against fashion, thereby opting out of the looking contest: "We fit the clothes with Spanx [body-shaping underwear], and then I didn't wear the Spanx for the show, so everything fits slightly wrong, it tugs a little bit." Hannah "always has one too many accessories, or an unflattering waistline." When Howard Stern offered her a backhanded compliment – "Good for her. It's hard for little fat chicks to get anything going" – Dunham repeated it on *The Late Show with David Letterman*: "I want my gravestone to say, 'She was a little fat chick and she got it going.'"

In an inversion of usual television practices, Hannah consistently beds men who are more beautiful than she is. Such is the strength of her point of view that we start to lose track of how beautiful she is. It is something we guesstimate, based on the responses of those around her. In season two, Hannah enjoys a brief affair with an attractive older doctor. "You're beautiful," he says.

"You really think so?"

"You don't?"

"I do. It's just not always the feedback that I've been given."

This episode, in which Dunham plays topless ping-pong, caused a flurry of online consternation. In *Slate* magazine, Daniel Engber wrote that "the episode felt like a finger poked in my guys-on-*Girls* eyeball, or a double-dog dare for me to ask, How can a girl like that get a guy like this?" Similar questions are rarely asked of Jonah Hill, or any of Dunham's male slacker contemporaries, but that presumably is her point. For someone who claims to be apolitical, Dunham knows how to push the misogynist buttons.

*

Laughter is mandated in the female, provided it is at the male's jokes. In this sense, humour is the reverse of beauty, which is adjudicated by men. But when laughter is withheld, it is the woman who is found wanting: she suffers from the female condition of humourlessness.

The 2011 hit film *Bridesmaids* was hailed as a "breakthrough" female comedy, affirming women's ability to make jokes that both men and women might laugh at. In response, A.O. Scott at the *New York Times* suggested that it was "being congratulated for settling an argument that nobody was really having." Except that many were having it, not least Christopher Hitchens in a (notably unfunny) piece for *Vanity Fair* in 2007. "Why are women, who have the whole male world at their mercy, not funny?" he asked. "Please do not pretend not to know what I am talking about." He nobly granted exceptions to women "who are hefty or dykey or Jewish, or some combo of the three." (Dunham, being half-Jewish and marginally hefty, might just qualify.) All other women are condemned to humourlessness, a sad fate in the Hitchens universe, wherein "wit, after all, is the unfailing symptom of intelligence."

Perhaps Hitchens was being *refreshingly politically incorrect*; perhaps he was *articulating a brave truth*. To question this is to risk being humourless about your own humourlessness. "For men, it is a tragedy that the two things they prize the most – women and humour – should be so antithetical." But would Hitchens truly have preferred the company of women who crack their own jokes rather than laugh at his?

Humour is a sexual asset for the unbeautiful man, but of less value to the unbeautiful woman. She can use her humour only to console herself; it has little worth in the sexual marketplace. In their 1995 dating manual, *The Rules*, Ellen Fein and Sherrie Scheider warned the would-be bride not to "be a loud, knee-slapping, hysterically funny girl. This is okay when you're alone with your girlfriends. But when you're with a man you like, be quiet and mysterious, act ladylike, cross your legs and smile."

Why should humour be discouraged in the young lady? Is it because cracking a joke is about doing rather than being? A joke that works exercises a particular type of potency: it engenders a physical reaction in your audience. Additionally, it implies you are not just being looked at, but are looking back. When Ellen DeGeneres was awarded "Sexiest Sense of Humor" by Victoria's Secret, she claimed to be "honoured to get this award because it's hard to be sexy and funny at the same time." She invited supermodel Miranda Kerr onto her television show to make the point. Clad in wings, a mini-dress and stilettos, Kerr breathed the word "cumquat," and performed a kittenish wink. The distinction could not have been clearer: Kerr was sexy; DeGeneres was witty. Humour would dispel the model's mystique: her eyes absorb light but remain unseeing. We do not look to her for subjectivity. The comedy in *Girls* is predicated on an uber-subjectivity, on Hannah's uncompromising vantage point. Few question the right of Seinfeld or Larry David to star in their own show, but many baulk at a young woman doing the same. "I think there is a self-deprecation or a humbleness that women are expected to have and it's unseemly other-wise," Dunham said to the *Atlantic*. "Philip Roth, to say he's the voice of his generation, everyone would be like, 'Obviously. Carry on, Philip Roth.'" Comparisons to Philip Roth might be overreach, but Dunham's use of "unseemly" is telling. *Girls* is above all a riposte to female shame: bodily shame, the shame of being on stage, the shame of being seen.

Like *Fifty Shades*, *Girls* has been tremendously popular among women, but it offers the pleasure of recognition rather than escapism. Much of the humour is *politically incorrect*, as Dunham savages contemporary mores. According to the rules of Gen-Y meta-humour, a simple innuendo about a *hole* would never suffice. The joke instead comes at the expense of the person making the innuendo, or the person offended by it, or both. When Hannah sabotages a job interview with a date-rape joke, the punchline lies not in the joke itself, but in the platitudes offered up by the interviewer: "Jokes about rape or race or incest or that sort of stuff, it's not *office okay*."

There is an unlikability to the characters of *Girls* which can extend to the series itself. Even this feels defiant, a flouting of the feminine expectation to ingratiate. Writing for the *Huffington Post*, the actor James Franco found the men the "biggest bunch of losers I've ever seen." He conceded that

> Lena Dunham gives the female characters just as many flaws as the guys. But the twist is twofold: we get to hear the girls' insider conversations, so we side with them against the men, and Lena is the ultimate creator, so no matter what she puts the girls through, she is always in control.

Franco successfully located the source of his disquiet: female subjectivity. Other critics were less sure. Some took exception to "nepotism" in the casting, to the fact that several of the actresses are descended from minor Hollywood royalty. Dustin Rowles suggested that the critical backlash "has less to do with the way they look, the fact they're unlikable, or nepotism (which isn't even a real issue), and has most to do with our disdain for privileged white people."

This may indeed be the case, but given that privileged white people exist, are their (our) lives ineligible subjects for art? And why was this criticism not extended to Girls' many precedents, ranging from Friends to Frasier? Could it be because white privilege here is regarded from a previously unsanctioned point of view: that of a young woman? And could this be related to the notion that women disqualify themselves from literary greatness by writing about female experience?

Surprisingly, much of this critique has issued from feminists who have found the series insufficiently inclusive. "Girls was supposed to be for the people, by the people," lamented Jenna Wortham. But who said? In episode one, Hannah suggests to her parents that "I think I might be the voice of my generation." But she rapidly qualifies it: "Or at least a voice. Of a generation." Dunham presents a viewpoint we have seldom seen on television; as a consequence we demand she represent us all. There are many ways to rob a woman of her subjectivity. Reducing her to her appearance is one of them; demanding she speak for an entire gender is another.

Feminism

There was one word noticeably absent from the misogyny speech, but which underpinned each of its sentences: feminism. In her Emily's List oration, Gillard observed that "the twentieth century was a century of big political movements and ideologies such as fascism, socialism and modernism. And yet the movement that outlasted them all, and surpassed them all in what it has achieved for humanity, is feminism – the struggle for women's emancipation and equality."

Before the misogyny speech, gender had not been a large part of Gillard's romance – as race had been to Obama, for instance. We all knew it was there, and projected the burden of our hopes or our hatred onto it, but she sidestepped its significance. She explained that "whatever the reasons, I never conceptualise my prime ministership around being the first woman to do this job. I conceptualise my job as being about delivering the things that make a difference for the nation."

Clearly, many do conceive of Gillard's prime ministership in these terms, from the misogynist to the feminist. While still a member of the shadow cabinet, Gillard acknowledged the pressure of this. "The feminist movement, women in the party, for a whole lot of absolutely good-hearted reasons are so happy to see a woman achieving that they are pretty keen to hold the pedestal aloft and make it even higher. So they are actually adding to the Golden Girl vortex themselves."

Any politician is by definition representative – of a faction, of a party, of an electorate – but we additionally demand of the female politician that she represent womanhood. The misogyny speech marked a moment when this worked in Gillard's favour: as she recognised, the speech gave voice to the experience of many women. And yet feminism is not a word she has frequently invoked. When asked, she and her female ministers identified themselves as feminists, though with some qualifications. "Content is more important than the word," Senator Penny Wong suggested, "and I worry a little that that sounds feminist can be used as a silencing or a limiting phrase."

According to the Oxford Dictionary, feminism is simply "the advocacy of women's rights on the grounds of the equality of the sexes." Why should that be silencing? And yet something so self-evidently reasonable has acquired a stigma, to the extent that "I'm not a feminist" has become a conversational trope.

The celebrity non-feminist had a big year in 2012. When presented with the Billboard Woman of the Year Award, the singer Katy Perry announced, "I am not a feminist, but I do believe in the strength of women." The former model Carla Bruni explained to French Vogue that

"I'm not at all an active feminist. On the contrary, I'm a bourgeois. I love family life, I love doing the same thing every day." Gwyneth Paltrow confessed to *Harper's Bazaar* that "this may not be feminist, but you have to compromise." She explained that if you want a family, "you have to be a wife, and that is part of the equation."

The young reader of a fashion magazine could well infer that feminism means eschewing a bourgeois life, doing something different every day, never compromising, and not being a wife. This confusion is partly the achievement of anti-feminist propagandists, through whose efforts a handful of adjectives attach themselves effortlessly to the word: *militant, strident, politically correct, humourless.* (All women are unfunny, but feminists especially so.) The image that has arisen is as terrifying as a Hun bayoneting a baby. The feminist is *angry.* She wishes to eliminate heterosexual inter-course, and maximise the world's abortions. She incinerates brassieres, and flies into a rage if a man opens a door. Probably she is hirsute as a Yeti, and harbours a vagina dentata. According to the American radio talk-show host Rush Limbaugh, she is a *Feminazi.* Worse yet: she is *unsexy.*

Certain radical feminists have lent support to such a stereotype. In her 1967 *SCUM Manifesto,* Valerie Solanas urged women to "overthrow the government, eliminate the money system, institute complete automation and eliminate the male sex." But the Feminazi is largely a propagandist invention. Monica Dux and Zora Simic described "straw feminist-bashing" as a "time-honoured anti-feminist tactic." If feminism can be turned into a beast, there is no need to engage with it. Less drastically, if feminist argument is diverted into endless discussions of door-opening, as on a recent episode of *Q&A,* everybody is bored into changing the channel.

None of this holds much appeal for our daughters, who partake care-lessly of feminism's victories while refusing to march under its banner. This leads to generational friction, and a recurrent chorus from second-wave feminists: "Ingratitude, thou marble-hearted fiend." Perhaps we should establish an annual day of feminist thanksgiving, in which we celebrate the achievements of the suffragettes and the second-wave feminists. As Gillard acknowledged, feminism has been the most transformative and enduring twentieth-century political movement. It is a measure of its success that we accept its gains as our birthright.

Is there a danger that we might give them away, through carelessness or cultural auto-correct? Feminism's stigma cannot be blamed entirely on the propagandists. It is a truism that feminists are very good at telling other feminists what they should think – almost as good as men. There is an implicit moral vanity in this: *my feminism is better than your feminism*, or even *my feminism is the one true Feminism*. Writing in *Slate*, Amanda Hess suggests that the question, "'Are you a feminist?' tells us much more about the feminist movement's own branding failures than it does the beliefs of the women prompted to respond." To adapt Groucho Marx, who would want to belong to a club that would not have them as a member?

In March this year, the Facebook executive Sheryl Sandberg released a book, *Lean In: Women, Work and the Will To Lead*. Part memoir, part self-help tome, part manifesto, it advises women to "lean in" if they seek career advancement. It does not attempt to solve female poverty, nor to bring down capitalism. Instead, it identifies some of the factors that might hold women back from positions of power. Sandberg believes that "more female leadership will lead to fairer treatment for *all* women."

The fact that Sandberg – from her position as a successful, rich woman – dared offer advice to other women provoked outrage. "She has a grandiose plan to become the PowerPoint Pied Piper in Prada ankle boots reigniting the women's revolution," wrote Maureen Dowd in the *New York Times*, maintaining that "people come to a social movement from the bottom up, not the top down." Joanne Bamberger in *USA Today* took similar umbrage at Sandberg's footwear, misrepresenting her position as "equality in the workplace just requires women to pull themselves up by the Louboutin strap." In the *Observer*, Yvonne Roberts rejected Sandberg's message on how to join the "alpha males' club" as "conservative and neoliberal and doesn't even pass as feminist." She accused Sandberg of having an "exceedingly plump" ego, because the book "is full of little strokes, such as mentioning that her family gets a lift in the private jet of eBay's chief executive and how wonderfully well her twenty-minute TED talk was received." Sandberg, in other words, violates the code of female self-deprecation. Ironically, this is something the book addresses: "Who would want to speak up when self-promoting women are disliked?"

Much of the spleen directed towards Sandberg is a version of that directed towards Dunham: *She is not speaking for all women, so how dare she speak at all?* Successful men share their stories of success; successful men are granted the privilege of individuality. Somewhere it was decided that a woman who claws her way to a podium must speak for us all.

Like denigrations of Obama as "a white man in black skin," criticisms of Sandberg's success cast her as a gender traitor. Regardless of one's views on Facebook or the corporate world, surely this is a self-limiting feminism. As Jessica Valenti, founder of the *Feministing* blog, wrote, "it assumes that any sort of success is antithetical to feminism. The truth is, feminism could use a powerful ally." There is a Russian joke about a meeting between two revolutionaries. "What are you fighting for?" asks the older one. "That there will be no more rich people!" comes the reply. The older revolutionary nods sagely. "Comrade, how things change. In my time, we fought for no more poor people."

Anxiety over privilege is as old as second-wave feminism. It stems partly from middle-class self-loathing, but also from the accurate identification of a blind spot. Yet insisting that any feminist must speak for all women is a great way to shut feminist conversation down. Angela Shanahan in the *Australian* has suggested that "the real obstacle with the language and the assumptions behind feminism is that women living in the rich, comfortable West in perfect equality with men simply don't believe it anymore. Some of us never have." Shanahan, we may remember, never thought misogyny was real either (clearly she is determined not to be gullible). There has never been a better place and time to be a woman, but are those of us inhabiting the rich, comfortable West really living in perfect equality with men?

First-world problem is a first-world expression, bandied about by those who partake blithely of first-world advantages. Alan Jones is a first-world problem. The internet troll is a first-world problem. There is an implicit privilege in being cyber-bullied, because it means you have a computer. None of us can "check our privilege" entirely. Demanding we solve poverty or female foeticide before we consider the gender imbalance of boardrooms is a recipe for paralysis. It implies that feminism is a zero–sum game, that there is not enough of it to go around. Like rejecting vegetarianism because you care more about the AIDS crisis, it becomes an excuse for non-action.

Feminism must be larger than *spot the misogyny*, but does this mean misogyny should go unremarked? Like sexism, it is most insidious when invisible. How is it that our porn stars identify a backlash many of us fail to see?

Eva Cox conceded to Dux and Simic that second-wave feminism "changed the structures but … didn't actually change the culture," but how do we change the culture? This is our unfinished business. Sandberg has been accused of *blaming the victim* with her suggestion that women can also change ourselves: by rejecting a script of compliance, by daring to ask for more. But surely the culture is our shared project. It is not only the invention of men. Like us, men are both its beneficiaries and its victims. In fact, masculinity can be a more restrictive straitjacket than femininity. Casting ourselves as victims and calling upon men to fix it only strips us further of agency.

A resilient feminism, surely, is a broad church. It can defy the stereotypes and be funny, as Greer and Moran have demonstrated in their different ways. For Moran, humour becomes the ultimate feminist weapon: "We just need to look [the patriarchal bullshit] in the eye, squarely, for a minute, and then start laughing at it." It can even be sexy, with a recent study in the *Sex Roles* journal suggesting that feminism boosts sexual satisfaction. It can also be deadly serious.

One of the messages of the misogyny speech is that we are not done with feminism yet. It has much to offer our daughters, even beyond equal

pay, the vote, bodily autonomy, the right to own property, the right to
have an education. It can offer them subjectivity – but it is up to them to
claim it. A liberation from the *she* of third person – that *she* who is to be
looked at, or tagged in Facebook, or poked with things, like a thing – into
that magnificent gender-neutral first person. I. Me.

SOURCES

1   "Labor had compiled material portraying Abbott as sexist": Nick Bryant, "The strategist: Julia Gillard's hard-nosed director of communications," *The Monthly*, December 2012 – January 2013, themonthly.com.au/issue/2012/december/1359520891/nick-bryant/strategist.

2   "it was clear that it was not 'essentially about herself'": Paul Kelly, "Reconciliation of the reckless and brave," *The Australian*, 12 December 2012, theaustralian.com.au/opinion/columnists/reconciliation-of-the-reckless-and-brave/story-e6frg74x-1226534887692.

2   "Alexander Downer interpreted this context": Alexander Downer, "PM whinges too much about her attackers – she needs to rise above criticism," *The Adelaide Advertiser*, 14 October 2012, adelaidenow.com.au/news/opinion/pm-whinges-too-much-about-her-attackers-she-needs-to-rise-above-criticism/story-e6freacl-1226495632037.

3   "Kevin Rudd claimed a similar folksy know-how": *Lateline*, ABC TV, 17 October 2012, abc.net.au/lateline/content/2012/s3613081.htm.

5   "Let us be clear: sexism is the daily routine": Louise Adler, "Enough is enough: it's time to leapfrog from the personal to policies," *The Age*, 8 January 2013, theage.com.au/opinion/politics/enough-is-enough-its-time-to-leapfrog-from-the-personal-to-policies-20130107-2ccq4.html.

6   "nobody in the real world thought misogyny was important": Angela Shanahan, "For the new feisty Gillard, misogyny is just so yesterday," *The Australian*, 30 March 2013, theaustralian.com.au/opinion/columnists/for-the-new-feisty-gillard-misogyny-is-just-so-yesterday/story-fn562txd-1226609085712.

6   "women have very little idea of how much men hate them": Germaine Greer, *The Female Eunuch*, McGraw-Hill, New York, 1971, p. 249.

6   "A few men hate all women all of the time": Germaine Greer, *The Whole Woman*, Anchor, London, 2000, p. 293.

6   "Anne Summers documented much of this": Anne Summers, "Her Rights at Work," annesummers.com.au/speeches/her-rights-at-work-r-rated.

7   "Gillard has experienced a degree of misogyny": Gerard Henderson, "Short-sighted see hate at every turn," *The Sydney Morning Herald*, 16 October 2012, www.smh.com.au/opinion/politics/shortsighted-see-hate-at-every-turn-20121015-27mx9.html.

7   "if Julia Gillard's supporters really believe": Gerard Henderson, "Policy, not gender, will decide Gillard's fate at ballot box," *The Sydney Morning Herald*, smh.com.au/opinion/politics/policy-not-gender-will-decide-gillards-fate-at-ballot-box-20130401-2h2zu.html.

7   "women perceived more criticism": Bernard Keane, "Tables turn on stumblebum Abbott as Labor cuts its error rate," *Crikey*, 5 October, 2012, crikey.com.au/2012/10/05/tables-turn-on-stumblebum-abbott-as-labor-cuts-its-error-rate/?wpmp_switcher=mobile&comments=50.

7   "Mr Abbott has been guilty of sexism": Annabel Crabb, "'Misogyny' misses the real malady," *The Sydney Morning Herald*, 14 October 2012, smh.com.au/opinion/politics/misogyny-misses-the-real-malady-20121013-27jn4.html#ixzz2QIv7Wb00.

8   "a note of wishful thinking in Nicola Roxon's response": Richard Willingham and Josh Gordon, "Dirt flies in Gellibrand pre-selection," *The Sydney Morning Herald*, 9 April 2013, smh.com.au/opinion/political-news/dirt-flies-in-gellibrand-preselection-20130408-2hhe7.html#ixzz2PvGOGwfX.

9   "we felt [Greer] was shadowing us": Monica Dux & Zora Simic, *The Great Feminist Denial*, Melbourne University Publishing, Melbourne, 2008, p. 4.

9   "genuine femaleness remains grotesque": Greer, *The Whole Woman*, p. 4.

9   "disgust is reason's proper response": Camille Paglia, *Sexual Personae: Art and Decadence from Nefertiti to Emily Dickinson*, Yale University Press, New Haven, 1990, p. 12.

10   "dumped or discredited with an intensity": Julia Baird, *Media Tarts: How the Media Frames Female Politicians*, Scribe, Melbourne, 2004, p. 1.

11   "Jones, with his ageing demographic": Amanda Lohrey, "A matter of context," *The Monthly*, November 2012, themonthly.com.au/gillard-and-press-gallery-matter-context-amanda-lohrey-6771.

12   "Abbott later admitted that 'I think a few people went over the top'": AAP, "Abbott says some at rally over the top," *The Sydney Morning Herald*, 24 March 2011, news.smh.com.au/breaking-news-national/abbott-says-some-at-rally-over-the-top-20110324-1c76c.html.

14   "Downer remarked on *Sky News* that 'I think it is disgraceful'": Lanai Vasek, "Abbott 'needs harder line against Labor,' says Alexander Downer," *The Australian*, 28 October 2012, theaustralian.com.au/national-affairs/abbott-needs-harder-line-against-labor-says-alexander-downer/story-fn59niix-1226504729211.

14   "after using the Minister for Innuendo": Paul Sheehan, "Gillard reveals true nature in playing gender card," *The Sydney Morning Herald*, 10 October 2012, smh.com.au/opinion/politics/gillard-reveals-true-nature-in-playing-gender-card-20121010-27cnq.html.

14   "playing the gender card is the pathetic last refuge": Miranda Devine, "Gender card is a loser for Gillard," *The Telegraph*, 14 October 2012, dailytelegraph.com.au/news/opinion/miranda-devine-gender-card-is-a-loser/story-e6frezz0-1226494961475.

15   "what women have understood 'gender card' slurs to mean": Julia Baird, "Words that millions of women have rehearsed, yet never spoken," *The Sydney Morning Herald*, 13 October 2012, smh.com.au/opinion/politics/words-that-millions-of-women-have-rehearsed-yet-never-spoken-20121012-27i1j.html#ixzz2Onqlt54H.

15   "within traditional institutions, success has often been contingent": Sheryl Sandberg, *Lean In: Women, Work and the Will to Lead*, Knopf, New York, 2013, p. 156.

16   "Downer accuses Gillard of 'whinging'": Downer, "PM whinges too much."

17   "Golden Girl vortex": Baird, *Media Tarts*, p. 184.

17   "That men should *do* and women should *be*": as Germaine Greer writes, "Women are the labouring sex," *The Whole Woman*, p. 128.

17   "I didn't worry about what I was going to *do*": Caitlin Moran, *How to Be A Woman*, Ebury Press, Sydney, 2012, p. 167.

17   "men 'like glory and bullshit'": Guy Rundle, "Maybe, just maybe, Obama had something on his mind," *Crikey*, October 5, crikey.com.au/2012/10/05/rundle-maybe-just-maybe-obama-had-something-on-his-mind/?wpmp_switcher=mobile&wpmp_tp=1.

18   "'to be feminist is to understand'": Greer, *The Whole Woman*, p. 8.

18   "Gillard is right to reject a cycle": Baird, *Media Tarts*, p. 184.

18   "'the liquid-metal cyborg'": Mark Kenny, "Simply put, Gillard is indestructible," *The Age*, 31 March 2013, theage.com.au/opinion/politics/simply-put-gillard-is-indestructible-20130330-2gzsb.html.

20   "a panel on 'politics and porn in a post-feminist world'": *Q&A*, ABC TV, 19 March 2012, abc.net.au/tv/qanda/txt/s3451584.htm.

20   "When Greer returned to *Q&A* in August": *Q&A*, ABC TV, 27 August 2012, abc.net.au/tv/qanda/txt/s3570412.htm.

22   "Hillary Clinton described it as the 'significance of the insignificant'" and "a veteran reporter quoted in Waldman's article": Ayelet Waldman, "Is this really goodbye?" *Marie Claire*, 18 October 2012, marieclaire.com/world-reports/hillary-clinton-farewell.

23   "confessed Gwyneth Paltrow": Prairie Miller, "Interview with Gwyneth Paltrow," *NY Rock*, November 2001, nyrock.com/interviews/2001/paltrow_int.asp.

23   "In 2001, a UK study found": "A woman becomes invisible at 46: that's the age when chivalry dies and grey hairs arrive," *The Daily Mail*, 30 June 2011, dailymail.co.uk/femail/article-2009427/A-woman-invisible-46-Thats-age-chivalry-dies-grey-hairs-arrive.html.

23   "women in their lateish fifties": Natasha Hughes, "Why do Australian women give up on their appearance?" *The Age*, 4 April 2013, theage.com.au/lifestyle/beauty/blogs/beauty-beat/why-do-australian-women-give-up-on-their-appearance-20130402-2h57z.html#ixzz2PYBMha52.

24   "The wolf whistles may have stopped": Tracy Nesdoly, "The invisible woman," *The Toronto Star*, 7 January 2012, thestar.com/life/2012/01/07/the_invisible_woman.html

24   "but for women it's a compulsory game": Moran p. 210.

24   "'What kind of impact does this coverage have?'": Baird, *Media Tarts*, p. 129.

25   "It is not until women learn to read": Greer, *The Whole Woman*, p. 185.

25   "a female username invites twenty-five times": "Study finds female-name chat users get 25 times more malicious messages," University of Maryland Department of Electrical & Computer Engineering, 9 May 2006, ece.umd.edu/News/news_story.php?id=1788.

27   "shocking, common and twelve years older": Nicola Formby, "My brunette blunder – 'The Blonde' loses her bottle," *The London Evening Standard*, 12 August 2009, standard.co.uk/lifestyle/health/my-brunette-blunder--the-blonde-loses-her-bottle-6711289.html.

28   "Beard claimed to be astonished": Mary Beard, "A Don's Life," *The Times Literary Supplement*, 27 January 2013, timesonline.typepad.com/dons_life/2013/01/internet-fury.html.

28   "a panel was convened on *Q&A* with a showbiz bent": *Q&A*, ABC TV, 28 May 2012, http://www.abc.net.au/tv/qanda/txt/s3507518.htm.

29   "a weapon even used by her beloved father": Nick Bryant, "What Gina wants: Gina Rinehart's quest for respect and gratitude," *The Monthly*, May 2012, themonthly.com.au/gina-rinehart-s-quest-respect-and-gratitude-what-gina-wants-nick-bryant-5024.

29   "'Barry Humphries' appearance on the ABC's *Q&A* program'": "Barry Humphries lets rip on *Q&A*," 29 May 2012, smh.com.au/entertainment/tv-and-radio/barry-humphries-lets-rip-on-qa-20120529-1zg9f.html#ixzz2PGZJych6.

30   "Geordie Williamson has observed the 'dolorous truth'": Geordie Williamson, "The competing sides of Clive James: the clown v. the critic," *The Monthly*, April 2013, p. 46.

31   "vacuous crap": Paul Murray, "Shame, ABC, shame," *The West Australian*, 2 June 2012, au.news.yahoo.com/thewest/a/-/news/13845914/shame-abc-shame.

31   "found it a 'farce'": Jeremy Sear, "Q&A: we've seriously nothing more important to discuss than Gina Rinehart's personal failings," *Crikey*, 29 May 2012, blogs.crikey.com.au/purepoison/2012/05/29/qa-weve-seriously-nothing-more-important-to-discuss-than-gina-rineharts-personal-failings.

31   "playground mobbing": Moira Rayner, "Lay off the Gina Rinehart fat attack," *Eureka Street*, 14 June 2012, eurekastreet.com.au/article.aspx?aeid=31807.

31   "The whole point of this *Q&A*": Peter Craven, "Controversial, funny, un-PC: the delights of a *Q&A* gone wild," *The Sydney Morning Herald*, 5 June 2012, smh.com.au/opinion/society-and-culture/controversial-funny-unpc-the-delights-of-a-qampa-gone-wild-20120604-1zs26.html#ixzz2PGfNQm87.

32   "damning graphs illustrating the discrepancy": VIDA: Women in Literary Arts, "The Count," 2010, vidaweb.org/the-count.

32   "women continue to buy more books than men": in 2012, women bought 62 per cent of all books sold: Bowker Market Research and *Publishers Weekly*, 2012 *US Book Consumer Demographics & Buying Behaviors Annual Review*, R.R. Bowker LLC, New Providence, 2012.

32   "[Mantel] was finally recognised as a literary heavyweight": Sophie Elmhirst, "The unquiet mind of Hilary Mantel," *New Statesman*, 3 October 2012, newstatesman.com/culture/culture/2012/10/unquiet-mind-hilary-mantel.

33   "she discussed Kate Middleton": Hilary Mantel, "Royal bodies," *London Review of Books*, Vol. 35, No. 4, 22 February 2013, pp. 3–7, lrb.co.uk/v35/n04/hilary-mantel/royal-bodies.

34   "astonishing and venomous attack": Francesca Infante, "'A plastic princess designed to breed': *Bring Up the Bodies* author Hilary Mantel's venomous attack on Kate Middleton," *The Daily Mail*, 19 February 2013, dailymail.co.uk/news/article-2280911/Duchess-Cambridge-plastic-princess-designed-breed-Booker-prize-winner-Hilary-Mantels-venomous-attack-Kate.html.

34   "even the *Guardian* found it to be 'damning'": "Kate, the 'plastic princess': Hilary Mantel's damning take on duchess," *The Guardian*, 19 February 2013, guardian.co.uk/uk/2013/feb/19/kate-duchess-cambridge-hilary-mantel.

34   "Mantel was 'completely wrong'" and "describing the remarks as 'pretty offensive'": "Cameron defends Kate over Mantel comments," *BBC News*, 19 February 2013, bbc.co.uk/news/entertainment-arts-21502937.

37   "digital immigrants": Mark Prensky, "Digital Natives, Digital Immigrants," *On the Horizon*, MCB University Press, Vol. 9, No. 5, October 2001, marcprensky. com/writing/Prensky%20%20Digital%20Natives,%20Digital%20Immigrants%20-%20Part1.pdf.

37   "Women are more active users of social media than men": "More women on Facebook, Twitter and Pinterest than men," Britney Fitzgerald, *The Huffington Post*, 9 July 2012, huffingtonpost.com/2012/07/09/women-facebook-twitter-pinterest_n_1655164.html.

37   "A York University study into Facebook usage": Soraya Mehdizadeh, "Self-presentation 2.0: narcissism and self-esteem on Facebook," *Cyberpsychology, Behavior and Social Networking*, Vol. 13, No. 4, 2010, pp. 357–364, people.uncw.edu/hakanr/documents/selfesteemandnarcissismonFB.pdf.

38   "we live in a culture of insta-celebrity": Jean M. Twenge and W. Keith Campbell, *The Narcissism Epidemic: Living in an Age of Entitlement*, Free Press, New York, 2009, p. 102. Twenge and Campbell cited a 2007 survey in which 55 per cent of American six- to nine-year-old girls say they use make-up.

39   "*Napoleon Perdis Nude Awakening look*": "Get the Napoleon nude look," lifestyle.com.au/style/get-the-napoleon-nude-look.aspx.

40   "shopping is presented to women as recreation": Greer, *The Whole Woman*, p. 143.

40   "Twitter 'speeds up the emergence of fashion trends'": "30 fashion Twitter feeds you shouldn't be without," 19 March 2009, hipsquare.wordpress. com/2009/03/19/30-fashion-twitter-feeds-you-shouldn%E2%80%99t-be-without.

41   "Female underarm hair started vanishing": Cecil Adams, "Who decided women should shave their legs and underarms?" 6 February 1991, straight-dope.com/columns/read/625/who-decided-women-should-shave-their-legs-and-underarms.

41   "Greer describes the high-heeled shoe": Greer, *The Whole Woman*, p. 312.

42   "American shock-jock Howard Stern remarked": Josh Kurp, "Howard Stern didn't mean to say *Girls* feels 'like a rape' because of Lena Dunham's nudity, you guys," *Warming Glow*, 15 January 2013, uproxx.com/tv/2013/01/howard-stern-didnt-mean-to-say-girls-feels-like-a-rape-because-of-lena-dunhams-nudity-you-guys/#ixzz2PN5HTOkR.

42   "'You've changed my life!' gushed Gwyneth Paltrow": Christina Valhouli, "Faster Pussycat, Wax! Wax!" *Salon*, 4 September 1999, salon.com/1999/09/03/bikini.

42   "Fanny VAT": Moran, p. 49.

43   "I can have a cake in the oven while I do a pole dance": Lenny Ann Low, "Jennifer Love Hewitt's 'vajazzling' invention," *The Sydney Morning Herald*, 12 March 2012, smh.com.au/lifestyle/celebrity/jennifer-love-hewitts-vajazzling-invention-20120312-1uteg.html#ixzz2PYt9sEf7.

43   "15 million plastic surgery procedures": Raya Jalabi, "Plastic surgery on the rise – with Botox and breast implants most popular," *The Guardian*, 30 January 2013, guardian.co.uk/world/us-news-blog/2013/jan/30/plastic-surgery-rise-botox-breast-implants.

43   "there is still something missing in their life": "Cosmetic surgery – vanity or something else?" motherinc.com.au/magazine/everything-for-mum/life-balance/selfdevelopment/432-cosmetic-surgery-vanity-or-something-else.

44   "woman with a nose that has a bulbous tip": Ellen Fein & Sherrie Schneider, *Not Your Mother's Rules*, Grand Central Publishing, New York, 2013, kindle edition.

44   "I love the shape and size of Kate Middleton's nose": Jacob E. Osterhout, "Seeking a royal sniffer: New York women rushing to get the Kate Middleton nose," *NY Daily News*, 13 March 2013, nydailynews.com/life-style/ny-women-rushing-kate-middleton-nose-article-1.1287848#ixzz2OVYyPqD8.

46   "a particular reality for women as an inferior class": Andrea Dworkin, *Intercourse*, Simon & Schuster, New York, 1997, pp. 122–124.

46   "304 scenes in popular pornographic videos": Ana J. Bridges et al., "Aggression and sexual behavior in best-selling pornography videos: a content analysis update," *Violence Against Women*, Vol. 16, 2010, p. 1065, g.virbcdn.com/_f/files/79/FileItem-273118AgressionandSexualBehavior2010.pdf

47   "similar acts are classified as 'non-violent'": Cordelia Fine, "The porn ultimatum: the dehumanising effects of smut," *The Monthly*, September 2011, themonthly.com.au/dehumanising-effects-smut-porn-ultimatum-cordelia-fine-3782.

47   "He started to spit on girls": Martin Amis, "A rough trade," *The Guardian*, 17 March 2001, guardian.co.uk/books/2001/mar/17/society.martinamis1.

47   "described by porn veteran Nina Hartley": in conversation with David Corlett & Maree Crabb, *Love and Sex in an Age of Pornography*.

48   "my whole reason for being in this Industry": Robert J. Stoller, *Porn: Myths for the Twentieth Century*, Yale University Press, New Haven, p. 31.

49   "Pussies are bullshit": Amis.

49   "It is easy to disappear when there are two penises entering you": Krissy Kneen, *Affection*, Text Publishing, Melbourne, 2009, p. 171.

50   "porn has become a central mediator": Maree Crabbe & David Corlett, "Eroticising inequality: technology, pornography and young people," *DVRCV Quarterly*, Vol. 3, Spring 2010, pp. 1–6, vwt.org.au/store/files/1295405361.pdf.

50   "That is where the market is taking us": Amis.

51   "gonzo porn now comprises 95 per cent of shoots": in conversation with Corlett & Crabbe, *Love and Sex in an Age of Pornography.*

51   "like De Sade's jilted aristocrats": Greer, *The Whole Woman*, p. 193.

52   "this new form of sexuality leads to isolation": reported in *The Italian Almanac*, italianalmanac.org'life'libido.htm.

52   "rigorously choreographed 'sex nights'": David Leafe, "Playboy mansion? More like a squalid prison," *The Daily Mail*, 30 December 2010, dailymail.co.uk/femail/article-1342643/Hugh-Hefners-Playboy-mansion-like-squalid-prison-say-Playmates.html.

54   "we 'parcel sexuality out'": Deborah L. Tolman, *Dilemmas of Desire: Teenage Girls Talk about Sexuality*, Harvard University Press, Cambridge, MA, kindle edition.

54   "Desire 'is one form of knowledge'": Tolman.

54   "Christina Aguilera sings": Tolman.

54   "Gaga is not there to be fucked": Moran, p. 260.

54   "Gaga, for all her writhing and posturing, is asexual": Camille Paglia, "Lady Gaga and the death of sex," *The Sunday Times*, 12 September 2010, thesundaytimes.co.uk/sto/public/magazine/article389697.ece.

55   "Why am I a slut and you're the player?": "Pink tells us: 'I'm just living my life. I don't want to be your kind of good," *Glamour*, June 2013, glamour.com/entertainment/blogs/obsessed/2013/04/pink-june-cover-excerpt.html.

56   "I don't think teens need to read about gratuitous sex": Jeffrey A. Trachtenberg, "Booksellers find life after Harry in a vampire novel," *The Wall Street Journal*, 10 August 2007, online.wsj.com/article_email/SB118670290131693667-lMyQjAxMDE3ODA2OTcwMDkyWj.html.

56   "ending of the romantic adventure": Leon F. Seltzer, "Evolution of the self," *Psychology Today*, 11 June 2012, psychologytoday.com/blog/evolution-the-self/201206/dominant-or-submissive-the-paradox-power-in-sexual-relationships.

57   "'it just happened' as a 'cover story'": Tolman.

57   "fantasy will often still be": Nancy Friday, *My Secret Garden*, Gallery Books, New York, 2008, p. 27.

58   "may be that power is not always that comfortable": Katie Roiphe, "Spanking goes mainstream," *The Daily Beast*, 16 April 2012, thedailybeast.com/newsweek/2012/04/15/working-women-s-fantasies.html.

58   "alpha holiday": Seltzer.

59   "in every orgasm there is domination or surrender": Paglia, *Sexual Personae*, p. 243.

59   "to feel some kind of ownership of your own body": Emily Nussbaum, "It's different for *Girls*," *New York Magazine*, 25 March 2012, nymag.com/arts/tv/features/girls-lena-dunham-2012-4.

60   "the episode felt like a finger poked": David Haglund & Daniel Engber, "Was that the worst episode of *Girls* ever?" *Slate*, 10 February 2013, slate.com/articles/arts/tv_club/features/2013/girls_season_2/week_5/girls_on_hbo_one_man_s_trash_episode_5_of_season_2_reviewed_by_guys.html.

60   "settling an argument that nobody was really having": A.O. Scott, "The funny-woman, alive and well," *The New York Times*, 28 May 2011, nytimes.com/2011/05/29/movies/bridesmaids-allows-women-to-be-funny.html?_r=0.

61   "Why are women, who have the whole male world at their mercy, not funny?" Christopher Hitchens, "Why women aren't funny," *Vanity Fair*, January 2007, vanityfair.com/culture/features/2007/01/hitchens200701.

61   "a loud, knee-slapping, hysterically funny girl": Ellen Fein & Sherrie Schneider, *The Rules*, Warner Books, New York, 1995, p. 19.

62   "Philip Roth, to say he's the voice of his generation": Alyssa Rosenberg, "*Girls*: a frank, funny look at 20-somethings, genital warts and all," *The Atlantic*, 11 April 2012, theatlantic.com/entertainment/archive/2012/04/girls-a-frank-funny-look-at-20-somethings-genital-warts-and-all/255744.

62   "Dunham gives the female characters just as many flaws": James Franco, "A dude's take on *Girls*," *The Huffington Post*, 30 May 2012, huffingtonpost.com/james-franco/girls-hbo-lena-dunham_b_1556078.html.

63   "our disdain for privileged white people": Dustin Rowles, "HBO's *Girls* and our resentment toward privileged, white America," *Pajiba*, 24 April 2012, pajiba.com/think_pieces/hbos-girls-and-our-resentment-toward-privileged-white-america.php#78rtx1sKfqBxfDT3.99.

63   "*Girls* was supposed to be for the people, by the people": Jenna Wortham, "Where (my) girls at?" *The Hairpin*, 16 April 2012, thehairpin.com/2012/04/where-my-girls-at.

64   "The feminist movement, women in the party": Baird, *Media Tarts*, p. 184.

65   "I'm not at all an active feminist": Ella Alexander, "Carla Bruni: feminism is unnecessary," *Vogue*, 27 November 2012, vogue.co.uk/news/2012/11/27/carla-bruni-dismisses-contemporary-feminism.

65   "this may not be feminist": Justine Picardie, "The real Gwyneth," *Harper's Bazaar*, March 2012, harpersbazaar.com/magazine/cover/gwyneth-paltrow-interview-0312.

65   "straw feminist-bashing": Dux & Simic, p. 6.

66   "Are you a feminist?": Amanda Hess, "Enough with the feminist police," *Slate*, 4 December 2012, slate.com/blogs/xx_factor/2012/12/04/katy_perry_says_ she_s_not_a_feminist_when_are_we_going_to_stop_asking_that.html.

66   "more female leadership will lead to fairer treatment": Sandberg, p. 185.

66   "the PowerPoint Pied Piper in Prada": Maureen Dowd, "Pompom girl for feminism," *The New York Times*, 23 February 2013, nytimes.com/2013/02/24/opinion/sunday/dowd-pompom-girl-for-feminism.html.

66   "women to pull themselves up by the Louboutin strap": Joanne Bamberger, "The new mommy wars," *USA Today*, 25 February 2013, www.usatoday.com/story/opinion/2013/02/25/the-new-mommy-wars-column/1947589.

66   "doesn't even pass as feminist": Yvonne Roberts, "Is Facebook's Sheryl Sandberg really the new face of feminism?" *The Guardian*, 17 March 2013, guardian.co.uk/books/2013/mar/17/facebook-sheryl-sandberg-lean-book.

67   "Who would want to speak up when self-promoting women are disliked?" Sandberg, p. 56.

67   "feminism could use a powerful ally": Jessica Valenti, "Sheryl Sandberg isn't the perfect feminist. So what?" *The Washington Post*, 1 March 2013, articles.washingtonpost.com/2013-03-01/opinions/37366536_1_sheryl-sandberg-jessica-valenti-vanity-project.

67   "the real obstacle with the language": Shanahan.

68   "changed the structures but ... didn't actually change the culture": Dux & Simic, p. 94.

68   "We just need to look [the patriarchal bullshit]": Moran, p. 14.

Andrew Charlton

I must admit to being a longstanding admirer of Mark Latham. Writing this now feels vaguely like a confession, but there was a time when I followed his career with great interest. Well before he became a political hard man, Latham was something of a policy wonk. As a young parliamentarian he wrote three books, a dozen essays and countless speeches. I was drawn to Latham because I found something in his writing I had never seen before: a smart young politician wrestling with the big questions.

Latham arrived in Canberra in 1994, during the fifth term of Australia's longest serving federal Labor government. Just two years later the party suffered its worst election loss in fifty years. For Latham, then still a freshman MP, the 1996 defeat was a political defibrillation. More than others, he understood its significance. Voters hadn't just changed their mind; they had changed their values. In the mid-1990s Australians had more money, more security and more education than ever before. Labor's base, the old working class, was developing into a new middle class: aspiring, consuming and wanting to choose what was best for themselves and their families. These voters had outgrown the crude collectivism of Labor's past. Unless Labor changed with them, it might never govern again except as an occasional stopgap between long-serving conservative administrations.

A new generation of progressive thinkers – including Latham, Tanner, Shorten and Rudd – set to work on the threshold question facing the modern Labor Party: what should the left stand for after the triumph of the market economy?

Latham threw himself at this question. He opened his first book, *Civilising Global Capital*, published in 1998, with a call to action that hit me between the eyes:

> Labor faces a task of fundamental reconstruction: returning its thinking to first principles … The economic restructuring of the 1980s in Australia has produced social and political restructuring

from which the ALP must devise a new political framework ...
Labor has no way back to the past ... [we] must rely on the politics
of transition – new circumstance, new thinking, new policies.

Civilising Global Capital is, to my knowledge, the most ambitious book ever
written by a sitting Australian politician. Latham spends most of the book playing Jenga with the Labor policy platform. In each chapter he withdraws, exam-
ines and then discards another axiom from the party's intellectual foundations.
His point was that Labor's traditional policies – welfare state, regulation and
industry policy – were losing their potency. Many modern social challenges –
including indigenous disadvantage, family breakdown, mental health and social
exclusion – cannot be solved with welfare cheques. And in a competitive global
economy, job security can no longer be guaranteed by government protection.
Latham urged the Labor Party to move away from "big government" policy
solutions, declaring that "social democracy needs to give closer consideration to
the relations between citizens rather than simply working from an assumption
that all social issues can be resolved in the state-to-citizen relationship."
   Latham's early writing is freighted with all the idiosyncrasies of an autodidact.
The language is bloated and overwrought, as if the young man is struggling to
wrestle complex argument into plain English. The prolificacy of his ideas often
creates a sense of disorder. From chapter to chapter he traverses the ages and
criss-crosses the political spectrum, weaving in concepts of Enlightenment philo-
sophy, musing on Hegelian theory and weighing in on Tony Blair's Third Way.
But his pages appeal because they throb with urgency and passion, his ideas are
original and his canvas is broad.
   In his second book, *What Did You Learn Today?*, Latham applies his thesis – that
government service provision must adapt to social change – to education policy.
As skills become more important in the workplace, "lifelong learning needs to
become Australia's national pastime" and education needs to extend beyond
schools and universities into "everyday life: in homes, in workplaces, in clubs,
in shopping centres, in libraries, in the places where people commonly come
together." Education is central to Latham's concept of equality – one of the traditional left-wing values he wants to modernise. Latham favours what he calls
"aspirational equality," where divergent outcomes are tolerated so long as they
are related to individual effort. Latham would later turn this idea into his famous
"ladder of opportunity" analogy; the role of government, he would say, should
be to provide equal access to the ladder, not to ensure that everyone ascends to
the same height.

Never again miss an issue. Subscribe and save.

☐ **1 year subscription** (4 issues) $59 (incl. GST). Subscriptions outside Australia $89.
All prices include postage and handling.

☐ **2 year subscription** (8 issues) $105 (incl. GST). Subscriptions outside Australia $165.
All prices include postage and handling.

☐ Tick here to commence subscription with the current issue.

PAYMENT DETAILS I enclose a cheque/money order made out to Schwartz Media Pty Ltd.
Or please debit my credit card (MasterCard, Visa or Amex accepted).

CARD NO.

EXPIRY DATE   /   CCV   AMOUNT $

CARDHOLDER'S NAME

SIGNATURE

NAME

ADDRESS

EMAIL   PHONE

tel: (03) 9486 0288 **fax:** (03) 9486 0244 **email:** subscribe@blackincbooks.com **www.quarterlyessay.com**

An inspired gift. Subscribe a friend.

☐ **1 year subscription** (4 issues) $59 (incl. GST). Subscriptions outside Australia $89.
All prices include postage and handling.

☐ **2 year subscription** (8 issues) $105 (incl. GST). Subscriptions outside Australia $165.
All prices include postage and handling.

☐ Tick here to commence subscription with the current issue.

PAYMENT DETAILS I enclose a cheque/money order made out to Schwartz Media Pty Ltd.
Or please debit my credit card (MasterCard, Visa or Amex accepted).

CARD NO.

EXPIRY DATE   /   CCV   AMOUNT $

CARDHOLDER'S NAME   SIGNATURE

NAME

ADDRESS

EMAIL   PHONE

RECIPIENT'S NAME

RECIPIENT'S ADDRESS

tel: (03) 9486 0288 **fax:** (03) 9486 0244 **email:** subscribe@blackincbooks.com **www.quarterlyessay.com**

Delivery Address:
37 LANGRIDGE St
COLLINGWOOD VIC 3066

No stamp required
if posted in Australia

Quarterly Essay
Reply Paid 79448
COLLINGWOOD VIC 3066

Delivery Address:
37 LANGRIDGE St
COLLINGWOOD VIC 3066

No stamp required
if posted in Australia

Quarterly Essay
Reply Paid 79448
COLLINGWOOD VIC 3066

The essays and speeches released in his 2003 book, From the Suburbs, see Latham hitting his stride as he draws his ideas together into something approaching a coherent whole. He focuses on reconciling left-wing values with an economy dominated by the market and a society dominated by individuals seeking self-determination. His solution is to recast government from "provider" to "facilitator." Governments can create opportunities, but individuals have to take some responsibility for realising them. Latham sees no contradiction here with traditional Labor values of equality and collectivism. Rather he claims that his "responsibility agenda" keeps faith with traditional working-class values of pride, effort and thrift.

From the Suburbs was the zenith of Latham's career as a Labor intellectual. Thereafter he began to transform himself from thought-leader to head-kicker as he ascended through the ranks of the parliamentary party. On the way up, his approach became steadily less thoughtful and more impulsive. He lost his academic idiom and adopted a crude, scatological vernacular. He called the prime minister an "arse-licker," referred to George Bush as the "most incompetent and dangerous president in living memory," and described his conservative opponents as "a conga-line of suckholes." By the time he became Opposition leader, he was a wholly different politician from the young intellectual I had come to know through his writing.

In the end Latham's parliamentary career adhered to the rule that nothing is so detrimental to political longevity than early success. After the 2004 election loss, he embarked upon a decade-long sulk that would prove many of his detractors right. His memoir, The Latham Diaries, was a remarkably honest and revealing portrait of the dysfunctions of modern politics. But Latham's compellingly candid critique – which should have sparked a national debate about the vagaries of media-driven personality politics – was lost in the wash of his own bitterness and vitriol. For years since, his columns in the Australian Financial Review have been venom-tipped darts, indiscriminately launched at his former colleagues.

*

I mention this background because it is impossible to understand Latham's recent contributions except as those of a man who is trying, intellectually and emotionally, to regain the promise of his younger self.

With this essay, Latham returns to the world of ideas. We are treated to a glimpse of the old Latham: the thinker. His voice has changed in recent years. The writing is now much cleaner than in his early works, and free of the personal agendas that ruined the Diaries. Occasionally he slips into hyperbole (he calls

Abbott a "rat-snake"), but for the most part this is the work of a strong mind, now unencumbered by the constraints of ambition and sectional patronage. There aren't enough of these minds in the ALP, and if Latham wants to return to this role, he should be welcomed back.

Many in the Labor Party now snigger at Latham, dismissing his regular public interjections as the fading gurgle of political failure. They should not be so smug. Latham tried – and perhaps is still trying – to rethink and refresh the post-Keating ALP. His fall from "promising intellectual" to "disillusioned has-been" is more than the sad story of one broken career; it is an allegory of Labor's failure to produce leaders and ideas capable of re-establishing the party's intellectual foundations in the post-Keating era.

Latham acknowledges he fell short of his mission: "We were tasked with revitalising the party's agenda after federal Labor's heavy defeat in 1996, but in large part, nearly two decades later, this goal remains unfulfilled." Reading Quarterly Essay 49 reminded me that Labor's next generation could do worse than pick up where the young Latham left off.

Andrew Charlton

Jim Chalmers

On the morning of 2 December 2003 a colleague and I were setting up a room in Parliament House for Kim Beazley's victory press conference, when a call came through to say that Mark Latham had instead won the caucus ballot to replace Simon Crean. We felt terrible for Beazley — a man I admire greatly and someone I went on to serve when he returned to the leadership — as we pulled down the logoed backdrop we had just constructed for him. He had fallen one heartbreaking vote short. On the thirty-first anniversary of Whitlam's election, it seemed at the time that the party was waving goodbye to the leadership generation that had sprung from the Hawke and Keating cabinets: Crean and Beazley at once. We know now it was an interregnum — of a sort.

The passage of time and the historical focus on the "Howard handshake," the resignation, the Diaries, the 60 Minutes stint in the 2010 campaign — all of these things have helped many forget the optimism in the party and the nation that Latham's leadership brought about. It was a white-knuckle ride, but for one exciting year it seemed Labor had found a sense of genuine purpose and verve. We appeared capable of replicating the conviction and courage that my generation of activists had arrived too late to experience under Paul Keating. Many of us devoured Latham's books and speeches, especially when they referred to busting up the old Tory establishment. We hung on his words, imagined that ladder of opportunity, and cheered him on as he frustrated our ageing nemesis, John Howard. To inelegantly adapt Milton Friedman and Richard Nixon, we were all Lathamites then.

He rose fast and high, then fell fast and hard, a victim of Prime Minister Howard's skilful fear campaign over higher interest rates, which proved in 2004 as effective as his asylum seekers scare in 2001. Latham retired to a property on the distant south-western fringe of Sydney to raise his kids. In the party (and in his diaries) there was disappointment and hate, recriminations and get-squares.

And now, after a decade-long winter, there are signs of a thaw in the animosity between Labor and its fallen leader. Not just Paul Howes's welcoming words at the National Press Club, nor even the recent stirring topics of his regular column (one of a dwindling number of must-reads each week in Australian journalism): searing critiques of Tony Abbott and the Tea Party-inspired right, and defences of Julia Gillard against the Slater & Gordon allegations. As well, a punchy and heartfelt response to Nick Cater's book *The Lucky Culture* for the Chifley Research Centre, Labor's think-tank.

But the most heartening sign yet is the title, tone and much of the content of another recent contribution, *Not Dead Yet*. It is hard to agree with every word (more on that later), and yet easy to see it as a well-written reminder that Latham remains an ideas machine on the centre left. That whatever the missteps of his political career – and he concedes they were many and substantial – he has something important to say about the ALP's future. Reading it gives you a sense that Latham, for so long accustomed to the accelerator, has found the steering wheel. Too late for his leadership, but just in time for the party he once led.

A useful way to understand Latham's essay, his new relevance to the conversation and the force of some of his ideas is by way of a former Venezuelan industry and trade minister and a former German deputy chancellor and foreign minister. This is not the beginning of a joke from the well-worn three-men-walk-into-a-bar genre, but a way to understand some of what Latham writes in his essay about the breaking down of the old structures of the left. Because, strangely, the Venezuelan, Moisés Naim, and the German, Joschka Fischer, help to tell Latham's story about Australian Labor's big challenges in the twenty-first century.

Naim is the author of a well-received recent book, *The End of Power*, which argues that "Being in charge isn't what it used to be." In the *Washington Post* essay which summarises his book, Naim relates a conversation in which Fischer said that when he was elected to government, "one of my biggest shocks was the discovery that all the imposing government palaces and other trappings of government were in fact empty places," and that "the imperial architecture of governmental palaces masks how limited the power of those who work there really is." In Naim's detailed and compelling assessment, strong forces around the world – such as the explosion of the middle class, global mobility and a cognitive transformation that values individual freedoms – are working to fragment power. As Naim describes it, "The More Revolution helps the challengers overwhelm the barriers, the Mobility Revolution helps them circumvent them, and the Mentality Revolution helps them undermine them," so that decision-makers in and out of politics have far less influence.

How is this relevant to Australian Labor? The fragmentation of the old structures of working-class life upon which its organisational and electoral hopes rested has thrown up the representational challenges Latham identifies in *Not Dead Yet*. He has the dichotomies right, between aspirationalists and the underclass, and between inner-city progressive elites and outer-suburban cultural conservatives. There is hardly a threat to Labor's future which isn't related in some way to these dilemmas, which Latham and others describe as serving two masters. Solving this constituent dilemma – aspirational/underclass and blue/green – is the ALP's philosophical and electoral Rubik's Cube. Getting all the colours to match up is proving its most daunting task.

For Lathamites, the frustration is that the fragmentation of constituencies and the dispersal of power was not supposed to play out like this. A decade ago, breaking up the influence of blocs was a Howard-era aspiration of Latham and his young charges. It was all about insiders and outsiders. The power of this image is demonstrated now by Tony Abbott's enthusiastic embrace of Cater's book about anti-intellectualism in Australia. A decade ago, Latham's goal was the fragmentation of the right-wing establishment, the devolution of power and influence to ordinary communities, out of the wood-panelled rooms of the Melbourne Club, and the prospect of policies to benefit the many over the few. A victory for the outsiders over the insiders, all of it serving Labor's historic mission: to enlarge the economy in a way that sees the benefits flow into a greater, not fewer, number of hands, as Wayne Swan would say today.

Instead, the fragmentation of power has disproportionately damaged the institutions of the left, while catalysing a rearguard action from the old institutional right, in the form of the Murdoch press, talkback radio and well-funded conservative think-tanks. Despite challenges to this institutional right from Clive Palmer, Bob Katter and their ilk, this Liberal–Murdoch–talkback triple whammy remains the dominant force on that side of politics. At the same time, Latham believes, the sensible centre has disappeared from the public conversation, as social media and other influences pushes contributions to the extremes. He is right to point to old power hubs which are decentralising, or else being bypassed by choosier, smarter people, leaving our democracy to what he describes elsewhere as a "wacky, whingeing wall of complaint." You see this in the decline of traditional media sources and the corresponding rise of new media. This creates the paradox of power dispersal in the new world – of expanding choice combined with a concentration of power in the fewer hands of those willing to participate in old-style representative politics in a meaningful, committed way. While Naim's "more, mobility, mentality" sends the mainstream elsewhere for its news and social participation, the old political battleground is dominated by two extremes: the Greens and Tea Party wannabes.

It is for this generation of Labor people and the ones that follow to deliver on Latham's welcome optimism that the ALP can fill the vacuum created in the centre of Australian politics by the changing nature of the media – at once fragmenting in the digital world as it consolidates into a few big outlets – and by the extremism of the right and the left. And there's enough that is good about his emphasis on environmental sustainability, educational reform, aspirational economics and concern for the underclass to make the essay essential reading, and to more than balance the points where I would take issue with Latham.

An example of where we differ is his charge that the ALP is confused on economics when, on the contrary, the past five years under Rudd, Gillard and Swan showed Labor at its decisive best, intelligently deploying the tools of Keynesian economic management to save Australia from recession. Those three contemporary politicians deserve the credit bestowed on them by one of the world's finest economists, Joseph Stiglitz, who described Labor's economic policies during the global financial crisis as among the best designed, best deployed, best timed stimulus programs in the world. But Latham shouldn't just take Stiglitz's word for it; consider what Latham's hero Paul Keating might have called a beautiful set of numbers, which show an Australian economy with low inflation, low interest rates, low unemployment, and growth that astounds many countries still waist-deep in the quagmire caused by the GFC. Latham's other writings point to these successes – especially rising living standards – without attributing them to the current crop of ministers. His beef is with the 1990s Crean–Beazley years that preceded his leadership rather than the Rudd–Gillard ones that followed him, but this is not teased out. Doing that would make his good essay even better, as would the recognition that implementing big policies on climate change and schools – Latham's stated priorities – over determined opposition are among the current prime minister's finest achievements.

But, to be clear, and to adopt Howes' and Latham's Christmas analogy, these are arguments in the family, to be settled over a beer. And they are ultimately healthy for the intellectual life of the party. Because Labor's recent achievements demonstrate that it isn't purpose that the ALP has been devoid of during the Rudd–Gillard years, but unity of purpose. Or perhaps there has been too much falling into the honey trap of personality-based, poll-obsessed politics that does not fuel the necessary generation of ideas. This needs to change if Labor is properly to address the dilemmas so thoughtfully sketched out in *Not Dead Yet*, weaving together the aspirationalists and the underclass, the blues and greens, and including new demographic groups into a coalition of the centre left capable of filling that sensible terrain of politics that Abbott, the whinging wall and sections of the media have now abandoned.

That means a Labor Party that is as good at hooking people up to the benefits of a vibrant, dynamic, aspirational economy in Asia as it was at protecting their jobs and communities when both were threatened by global economic madness. It means helping people take two steps from poverty – from welfare-dependent underclass to working class to aspirational class – rather than just one, and representing each group without relying solely on the old institutional left. It means understanding that the collectivism of the labour movement was not just defensive, but aspirational, created to give working people access to the lives and labour conditions that the better-off got by right. It means harnessing the tools of the new media and new economy to shape breakneck demographic and technological change to Labor's advantage. In short, it means delivering the powerful egalitarianism that Latham hankers for, in his old *and* new incarnations, making the dispersal of power that Naim describes work for Labor and middle Australia, not against it.

Jim Chalmers

| | Correspondence

Peter Brent

Mark Latham has many qualities, but as a political strategist he was and remains ordinary. His Quarterly Essay may or may not contain sound prescriptions for reform of the Labor Party and policy ideas (in particular, he has long been persuasive on the part played by norms and role models in economic and social deprivation), but on the politics Latham's pen is decidedly impressionistic.

Romanticising the Hawke–Keating governments is almost de rigueur in contemporary political analysis, but Latham's characterisation is more one-dimensional than most. And unreal to anyone who was following politics during that period – which, of course, would include him.

Like many historians, Latham seems a willing captive of the prism of the present and the demands of the narrative. This makes for a rollicking story, but the lessons can be disastrous if actually implemented as strategy. His time as Opposition leader in 2004 was like that: sometimes it seemed as if emulating the key themes of Gough Whitlam's 1972 victory – and getting commentators to see him in these terms – would push history to repeat itself.

It's true that Keating was largely responsible for the increased economic literacy of the nation, in part via the press gallery. By the late 1980s it seemed everyone knew about the current account problem and the fact that the world didn't owe us a living. But the 1980s economic reforms driven, as Latham would have it, by Keating's own life experiences? Keating in the Labor tradition of "community engagement"?

In reality many of those prescriptions came from the bureaucracy and were fashionable in certain circles around the globe, which was why they came to be put in place in several countries. Importantly, most of the new agenda was supported by the federal Opposition of the day, who if anything complained it didn't go far enough. Yes, Bob Hawke and Paul Keating possessed greater political courage than their successors, and then John Howard had more than his successors, but Hawke and Howard were also accused of timidity at times, of being overly influenced by opinion polls and focus groups.

Latham greatly favours Keating over Hawke; we read of the "Keating legacy of micro-reform and productivity growth," "Keating's creation of a 'miracle economy'" and repeated references to the "Keating settlement." But "economic rationalists" much preferred Keating the treasurer – under Hawke – to Keating the prime minister, and his one election win in the top job, in 1993, was a blow against the kind of economic reform he (and Latham) now describe him as the architect of.

Hawke and Keating were successful politicians, so they would say one thing during an election campaign and then, after being re-elected, do another. Sometimes a Coalition policy they warned would be disastrous to the fabric of Australian society came to be implemented by them later. If there are lessons from that period in office, it's that the ALP under Hawke won a highly winnable election and then didn't look back. It never doubted it belonged in office. Like all governments, what it did in government bore little resemblance to what it promised in opposition.

Others may have fretted about what it meant to be "Labor," but members of the Hawke and Keating governments were too busy pulling the levers of state. They were proudly different to – they reckoned they were easily better than – earlier Labor governments. Compare that with today's politicians and commentators – like Latham – who obsess about past glories. But after it was all over in 1996, it became apparent that a hollowing-out of the party, particularly at membership level, had also been taking place.

Some of Latham's advice is wishful thinking at best and simple fiction at worst. "When financial issues are dealt with at arm's length, it creates room in the daily media cycle for Labor to emphasise its other progressive reforms, such as social initiatives and action on climate change." That must have tripped easily off the keyboard.

Or: "Labor would be better served by initiating a mature, factual debate about the limits of economic policy. It needs to explain to the electorate how the role of government has fundamentally changed." I think I read that scene in the book *Primary Colors*.

Latham advocates a closer identification with the politics of climate change, because, it seems, in several decades history will pronounce the party correct. But, as with Labor's opposition to the Vietnam War and its awful drubbing at the 1966 election, eventually ending up on the right side of history does you a fat lot of good today.

Again in line with most commentators, Latham conflates a large and active party membership with electoral success. But if the two have a relationship, it seems, from the historical record, to be inverse. Back in the first half of last century, when membership was at its highest, federal election wins were scarce. At state level the party's greatest collective success – including in some states the biggest wins or longest periods in office – came only recently, five to fifteen years ago, when membership was already on a downward spiral. And (sorry to bring them up again) if anyone is responsible for the decline in membership, it's the sainted Hawke and Keating, whose policies members found so offensive. Had they listened to members more, they probably wouldn't have lasted so long in office. (This is the problem with any plan to empower the membership.)

Latham writes of the "core delusion of 21st-century democracy, that political parties can fragment and hollow out, yet still win the confidence of the people." Now he's getting somewhere, but it applies as much to the Liberals as to Labor, and (to varying degrees) to their counterparts overseas.

The thing we call "democracy" seems to have evolved this way in countries like ours. The electorate is bypassed in a technocratic consensus, with certain policies – on immigration and deregulation – implemented regardless of who is in power. With hindsight many or most voters end up agreeing it was good for them after all, but it's not surprising that the number of people loyal to either side of politics continues to decline. The product of this could be seen a decade ago, when the Liberal and National parties were recording record-low primary votes at state elections. Now the ALP is, and the records are even lower.

Like the best political storytellers, Latham doesn't believe in the electoral cycle, but it is real and is the reason state Labor governments have been crashing over the last five years.

One day Australia's two-party system might break. If it happened today, the ALP would shatter, but if it happens in five or ten years' time, it might be the conservative parties. Increasing party membership won't stop that.

Peter Brent

Russell Marks

Labor parliamentarians have long contributed to what can be called the "Fabian genre" of Australian publishing. Generations of ALP politicians – past and present and future – sketch their visions of progressive, social-democratic political reform in well-researched, often book-length monographs on contemporary problems and solutions, continuing into the new century. Barry Jones, Gareth Evans, Andrew Theophanous, Lindsay Tanner and Wayne Swan are among the most recent published authors in the Fabian genre. Mark Latham was an important contributor with *Civilising Global Capital* (1998) and *From the Suburbs* (2003).

The Fabian genre has two defining features: a commitment to social justice and social-democratic reform; and bona fide attempts at social and cultural analysis from a social-democratic perspective. But since about 2006, the Fabian genre has mysteriously gone missing. Recent contributions from Labor writers have been devoid of social analysis. Tanner's *Sideshow* (2011) decried the impossibility of progressive reform politics in the contemporary media cycle without referring once to the socialist theorists who have long warned of the distorting effects of the profit-driven media corporations. None of the contributors to a 2010 collection of essays, *All That's Left: What Labor Should Stand For*, made any attempt to develop a theory of power, and the questions of what the party should do about special economic interests, the American alliance and the party's own factional warlords were not addressed at all.

Meanwhile an alternative genre of Labor writing has come to the fore, one which dates back at least to Gordon Childe's 1923 dismissal, in *How Labour Governs*, of the parliamentary ALP as middle-class liberals who would ultimately sell out their working-class base when the crunch came. Latham and Bob Carr have called this Labor's vampire genre. Rodney Cavalier's *Power Crisis* (2010) and Tanner's latest book, *Politics with Purpose* (2012), fit within it. Latham himself can be credited with reviving the genre with the publication of his *Diaries* in 2005.

With *Not Dead Yet*, Latham purports to return to the Fabian tradition of proposing solutions. He suggests that Labor should revive the educative function it adopted so successfully in the 1930s and '40s, and then the late 1960s and the 1980s. He proposes that climate change should be Labor's "great disruption," the single issue which allows it to dominate the political airspace as against the right's anti-scientific denialism. He makes a strong argument for primary pre-selections. And he nominates the increasingly entrenched underclass as the true target of the party's poverty-alleviation goals. On these points, one can hardly disagree. His analysis of what he calls the "new right" is in equal parts amusing and terrifying.

But Latham's is a curious Fabianism. Since Paul Keating, it has not been uncommon to hear Labor politicians parrot the dictates of the market-fundamentalist economists Friedrich Hayek, Milton Friedman and James Buchanan. But it is rare to see them go to such uncritical lengths in print. Never mind the confused "Third Way" politics of Tony Blair and the 1990s; much of Latham's essay is pure, unabashed neoliberalism. He denounces unionists as "rent-seekers" whose arguments for greater protections for workers are special pleadings, which in practice work to reinforce their own power and privilege at workers' expense. He claims that "what's good for capital investment in the economy is also good for employment levels, wages and working conditions." His proposed education "reforms" are pure Hayek: assess the students and performance-manage the teachers to within an inch of their measured lives and expect the mountains of quantitative data (and the consequent swelling of administrative power) to have some kind of magic effect on "educational outcomes." He writes, à la Thatcher, of "economic realities" and the futility of "any other approach" to economic policy-making than that of what he cleverly calls the "Keating settlement."

In *The End of Certainty*, Paul Kelly's famous account of the 1980s, the "Australian settlement" (comprising White Australia, economic protection, loyalty to the British empire, government intervention and industrial arbitration) was broken apart by Keating's introduction of IMF-sanctioned reforms, which ultimately made Australian life much more unsettled. There were higher economic returns for successful entrepreneurs, but the shifting of the burden of risk from the state to the individual produced many losers too. An increasingly entrenched under-class has risen commensurate with the so-called free-market reforms. Latham believes this can be effectively dealt with by a policy of "dispersal" – of scattering public housing throughout every neighbourhood rather than concentrating disadvantage in high-rise blocks and poor suburbs.

Let the free market rip, and then ameliorate the disadvantage with targeted government programs. That is Latham's strategy in a nutshell. But his policy of "dispersal" would run into problems of its own. Now that the ethic of "choice" is available to parents of schoolchildren, they increasingly exercise that choice by pulling their progeny out of government schools and into sites of concentrated advantage – the private colleges. That is, if they can afford to. Government schools are increasingly where children of parents who can't afford private schools are sent. They become sites of concentrated disadvantage. Australia is rapidly returning to an education system which reproduces the existing class structure: in any given suburb, the poor kids go to the state schools and the rich kids go to the private schools. Such a division would render a policy of dispersal irrelevant.

The reproduction of the existing class structure was the function of nineteenth-century education systems, and it's hardly surprising that the nineteenth century was also a time of fundamentalist belief in the undisputed benefits of a so-called free market. But wait, Latham proclaims: economic liberalism does in fact produce benefits for all, which trickle down to even the poorest.

This is the claim at the heart of Latham's essay: that the free-market reforms of the 1980s have been good for almost everyone. He even quotes sources in evidence and believes them without question. But this claim is actually hotly contested, on two main grounds. First, while it's inarguable that *average* wealth and incomes have increased, there's much data which shows that the vast majority of that growth has been concentrated in the top ten per cent. Other NATSEM reports directly contradict its *Prices These Days* report, upon which Latham relies exclusively. At best, neoliberal economic policies have zero redistributive effect; at worst, wealth is further distributed away from the poor and towards the wealthy. Even if the poor have become wealthier in real terms, we know that the most meaningful measure of an economically wealthy society's health and happiness is its level of inequality. It's a curious Fabianism which is comfortable with rising inequality.

Second, and even more significantly, Latham cannot see the nexus between the IMF's neoliberal "reforms" and the increasingly individualistic focus on economic wealth to the exclusion of all else. One of the failures of the neoliberal experiment has been its insistence that human happiness can be measured by GDP growth. To a point, sure; past that point, we seem to become hoarding Scrooges, counting every hard-earned penny lest it be stolen by the tax office to pay for the education of someone else's child.

Latham claims that post-Keating Labor has been a victim of its own success. It's a curious "success" for a social-democratic political party which sees its policies remould citizens into wealth-aggregating "econozens" whose only ideology is consumerism.

In *Not Dead Yet*, Latham repeats the old fallacy of the Third Way: to expect that one can use the tools of the right for social-democratic ends without in the process becoming affected by that use. Think of computers: no tool is purely instrumental; they change us, too, as we use them. It is a fundamental misreading of Keating's micro-economic "reform" agenda to think that it is not implicated in the decline of leftism, unionism, progressive communalism and even social democracy itself.

Most curiously of all, Latham insists that we listen only to the dictates of the NSW Labor Right – the faction which has denuded modern Labor of any substantive social democracy and allowed it to become a vessel for the political and commercial advancement of ambitious numbers men.

Latham's analysis of modern Labor is all wrong. The problem is not that there's not enough neoliberalism; it's that there's too much. Its social democracy is only occasionally articulated – as in Rudd's *Monthly* essays – but never in the end acted out, because the party now lacks a workable theory of power which would allow it to take on vested economic interests in the name of the common good. Such a theory was what Labor traded away during the 1980s in pursuit of the IMF's free-market reforms. Since then, the party has been characterised by an identity crisis of truly existential proportions: should it continue to embrace the "reforms" that made Australia richer but handed power to business at the expense of organised labour, or should it emphasise social democracy once again? To continue to pretend that it can do both will only lead to more confused and ultimately ineffectual policy-making of the kind that has characterised the Rudd–Gillard executive, while the suburban "econozens" are attracted by the Liberals' populism and the educated middle class continue to drift to the Greens.

Russell Marks

Guy Rundle

When the author of *Not Dead Yet* rose to prominence in Australian politics in the 2000s, it appeared that there would be two prominent Lathams in Australian political history, Mark joining Sir John Latham who, in the 1920s, came as close as anyone to dismantling the centralised wage-fixing at the heart of the Australian settlement. In more recent years I've come to conclude that there are two Lathams within Mark Latham himself. One is someone determined to think deeply about what the good life would be in modernity, what we should aim for, and how to reconstruct a progressive politics to achieve it. This is the Latham who began his *Diaries* somewhat bluff and bumptious about the dynamic and positive powers of the market, and ended them, one scarifying election later, driving through Sydney's western suburbs, disturbed by the appearance of the fortress-like McMansions, families walled in from each other, living off cable television rather than communal life, and Latham sounding for all the world like the judgmental leftists he had hitherto criticised, Adorno in a Monaro. He understood something then, about what happens to a society with privatised prosperity, and the dilemmas it creates for a mass progressive party.

There is some of that in the essay, but there is also the other Latham, the somewhat simplistic marketophile, advocating policies based on thin evidence that purport to be based on non-ideological problem-solving, but are really the projection of a pretty fixed idea of human life and Australian society – and this limits the usefulness of the essay for the reconstruction of Labor as a progressive party.

Indeed there were times reading it when I recalled the story of Bernard Shaw meeting Sam Goldwyn, when the former undertook a lucrative screenwriting deal. Goldwyn rabbited on about theatre and ideas, only to be interrupted by Shaw remarking, "The trouble with you, Mr Goldwyn, is that you want to make art; I want to make money." As someone from the left that Latham defines himself against, I want the ALP to be a viable mass political party, capable of winning elections and advancing a steady and realistic progressive platform, giving people the opportunity for better lives. I thought Latham's essay would be in that spirit, and a corrective to Clive Hamilton's Quarterly Essay 21, *What's Left?*, which wanted the ALP to be a crusading left social-democratic party on a macro level, well out of kilter with the way average Australians think about their lives. Latham presents his marketophile policies as if in answer to a popular demand, when they ought rather be presented as a personal preference.

Latham correctly identifies a core problem for Labor, the decomposition of its class base into subclasses with divergent interests. Hitherto, the unemployed were simply the usually employed currently without a job (even when, during the Depression, that was 25 per cent of them).

Now, prosperous trades and service/care workers have income and assets dividing them utterly from the minimum-waged, dividing those in turn from ongoing welfare recipients. Policies that once simultaneously tackled inequality and improved the mass of people's lives are now split; what addresses inequality often disadvantages the high-waged with extra costs. Tackling inequality among various subclasses must either be done by appealing to a universal interest and obligation – just as society is becoming steadily more atomised – or be "smuggled in" under cover of policies addressed to a prosperous majority. Since it is the majority policies by which the ALP lives or dies electorally, I'll focus on those.

Latham's argument, as I understand it, is that Labor should reaffirm its successes in creating a market-driven economy by attacking various myths – such as a cost-of-living squeeze – head-on, and should then advance a social policy for aspirationals, with education and opportunity expansion at its core. His suggested mantra for this reorientation is, "What would Keating do?"

Well, maybe. But I have to admit that some of this is more reminiscent of late Keating – the Keating of, "What are people going on about?" and of kissing the ground at Kokoda to try to change the way Australians understood their history. The dual problem here is that if you're going to attack a widely held myth with statistics, you better make sure there's no reality to the myth. And you better not mistake your own myths, such as "aspirationalism," for an unquestionable reality.

Most people want better lives, for themselves and their children and those close to them – but the idea of "aspirationalism" is a very particular and rigid rendering of it. As Latham constructs it, it has a relentless quality, a ceaseless advancement to it, expressed in accumulation and grim Tiger Mother-style education for the kids.

That social vision is advanced by most of the current ALP elite past and present, whatever their other differences. Of course it is. They're all driven people, members of a lifelong political caste, and they project that assumption onto the general electorate as the only way to live your life. There seems to be no understanding that most people don't live that way; that's why they're most people, the average, by definition. The idea of a better life encompasses many incommensurable things – not merely better houses and material things, but more free time, more family time, ease of life, security and a certain centredness in their own existence. Past Labor leaders understood this, and so did John Howard – he took it over by telling people they should be able to feel more "comfortable and relaxed." That wasn't just about Keating's perceived advancement of a cultural liberal agenda; it was about the sense Labor had established in the early 1990s that everyone was on a forced march from the suburban "Settlement" society established over a century to … God knows where. Bob Hawke had kept a lid on such enthusiasm, won four elections (and is unmentioned in Latham's chronicle of leaders); Keating ramrodded it and lost the farm. In the ensuing years, elements of the NSW Right have developed an enthusiasm for the market that amounts to a repudiation of the mixed society/economy that made this country one of the best places to live a working/middle-class life in the twentieth century.

This vision leads to some flat-out absurdities: "Four years later [after the 2008 crash] history's verdict is still clear: open, free markets work better than any leftist alternative." No, they don't. The most successful societies are the north European social democracies, enterprising but secure, poverty all but abolished, inequality – class, gender, race – relentlessly attacked. IKEA, H&M, Volvo – three global brands from a semi-socialist society. Name three Australian equivalents. Elsewhere, Latham argues that no technical innovation has come from the state, which is sheer embarrassing ignorance: try the computer, antibiotics, the jet, the agricultural green revolution, the internet and the web, for a start.

Such marketophilia is clearly delusional, and so too is the notion that things will be improved by equating "aspiration" with the desired good life. Combining the two in an education policy creates an evidence-free policy prescription for social betterment. In noting the models of educational success, Latham mentions Finland – but only in passing and on the way to some grim Asian-style vision of relentless work, parental cooption and ruthless competition. No wonder: because in creating the best education system for a European-based culture, Finland has eschewed everything Latham suggests. Schools have shorter hours, later starts in life, no performance assessment for teachers, conditions that the

Australian Education Union could not hope for even at its most militant, and *a lack of* parental involvement. Why isn't this canvassed as a possible model? Because it is recognisably leftish, I suspect. Latham's education prescriptions, which have a slightly crankish specificity, are in service to his idea of how he would like the culture to be, rather than how it is. Most importantly, it is contradictory at its core. He wants a market-driven culture that maximises individual autonomy — and then to penalise financially parents who don't help with their kids' homework. Yeah, that's a vote-winner. Thank God we've abandoned statist paternalism.

This is presented as a prescription for Labor, but it's really a restatement of its current failure. This is what people really, really hate about the ALP at the moment: the simultaneous insistence on an ever more testing market economy from the right, and a left that has decided to identify itself with micromanaging behaviour, à la plain cigarette packaging. What makes it even more comical is that — as the party heads towards a 28 per cent primary vote — its grandees walk around telling each other how they've got their finger on the pulse of the electorate. As with Michael Costa, Cassandra Wilkinson and other marketophiles in higher places, it is difficult not to feel that the ancient enemy is, as always, the ALP Left, and that that epic struggle dictates a politics which is then presented to the Australian public as "what they want." Sometimes this verges on the sycophantic. The idea that trying to get Gina Rinehart and others to cough a little more in tax is some sort of attack on free enterprise is pretty pathetic. May as well wind up the party entirely, if that's the red line.

This is all a pity, really, because the other Latham recognises the central dilemma for a rational, progressive party: that it must respond to people's desire for more individually expansive lives even as it prepares for the civilisational challenge of climate change effects. The answer for such a party is surely to listen to what people want, and focus on the things that joint the present to the future. Leaving aside old left–right battles, that is surely about addressing what people are complaining about when they talk of cost-of-living pressures. Australians are squeezed in a wider sense: ludicrous house prices, poorly designed cities, overpriced (private) services, free-time poverty, etc. Surely what bridges us to a climate change society are policies that open up real choices in people's lives — affordable good housing, more flexible work, support for social caring roles, child care and better parental leave options, multi-life-stage higher education — offered not as coercive impositions, but as real alternatives to a parallel high-consumption lifestyle. Modest, targeted, realistic policies that centre on the ALP's support base and don't get distracted by what cannot be regained (the IT crowd, whom Latham hymns as aspirational, vote Greens at a rate significantly higher than the general public; Latham and others better get used to the idea that the Greens will grow as the information class grows, and this change will eventually deliver them an inner-city Lower House base). From the left, I'm suggesting a politics conformed to where the Australian public is. So sometimes is Latham, and one would like to see more of him. Sadly, this essay was mostly written by the other Latham, the engineer/brand manager of human souls, pushing markets and Mem Fox readings on a public that want something more.

Guy Rundle

Louise Tarrant

Mark Latham — like the commentariat generally — has utterly failed to listen to the millions of workers who provide essential services in areas like child care, aged care, cleaning, security and hospitality. Their voices need to be heard before they are written off as relics of the past.

"I don't think my family should have to sweat, freeze or live in darkness because we can't afford power," says Reena from country New South Wales. Or Allan, struggling to pay bills and meet his family's needs: "I have to work forty-five plus hours a week to pay the bills, and all I want is more time with my family." Netta's concern is insecure employment: "My job is not secure like the way it once was and that is a big concern to me." And for Andrea, housing is the big challenge: "The rent takes half my wages every week, so it is really hard to survive." These are the excluded voices from Latham's analysis and increasingly the disengaged from our daily politics.

According to Latham, "As the working class has splintered, most of Labor's constituency has climbed upwards in society, while a residual cohort has fallen back." You belong to either the "aspirational class," characterised by entrepreneurial activity or "clean, creative professional jobs," or you are part of the "underclass," reliant on welfare.

Reena, Allan, Netta and Andrea, working desperately hard to provide for themselves and their families, fall through the cracks of the Latham typology. Nowhere in his essay are these workers and their families' experiences understood or given voice. Their concerns are dismissed by reference to a narrow analysis of income growth. Fragmented jobs, burgeoning debt, insecure lives, shifts in cost and risk from the state and private sector onto individuals, and wealth concentration, all go unmentioned.

So how do we better give voice to these experiences? How do we ensure political leaders and commentators like Latham understand and are responsive to these real stories and concerns? Historically the ALP, through its partnership with unions, has been the political vehicle for this.

Latham suggests this purpose is no more: "The ALP's original purpose, the mass participation of working men and women in parliamentary democracy, has dissolved." He then goes on to advocate a complete fracturing of the relationship between the party and unions.

Not surprisingly, a flawed analysis leads to a flawed prescription.

Instead of a fracturing we should be looking for a re-engagement between Labor and its base of working people. Labor is soulless and rudderless without a connection to working people. Yes, the party has to reach out to broad sectors of the community to build a vibrant and dynamic membership, but why are people like Latham so quick to dismiss the hundreds of thousands of union members who – through their unions – bring real voices and values to the party? The challenge is in strengthening that connection, not minimising or dismissing it.

This re-engagement is key to Labor's future fortunes but also key to responding to a growing democratic deficit in our country, as many workers turn away from politics. They see the political process as disconnected from their own lives and aspirations.

How do we bridge this distance and transform it into something that reflects and speaks to working people? That is the very real challenge for unions and the Labor Party. It is a challenge United Voice is not just talking about, but also doing something about. We have embarked on a new course – Real Voices for Change – to try to create greater opportunities for members to tell their stories and understand that their own experiences are often shared by others. In the past six months we have reached out to all of our members and so far 26,000 of them have shared their stories and presented ideas for change. A new member leader group will begin meeting from July to distil these ideas, engaging members as they go. Already these conversations have thrown up a wealth of information, ideas, conundrums and commitments to become more involved. We'll build on this and these members will help redefine and reposition our union. We need to take these voices and activists into the Labor Party to invigorate and re-animate it as well.

Latham states: "The working class has gone the way of record players and typewriters – a social relic irrelevant to the future shape of the Labor movement." He is simply wrong. The working class has not disappeared – in articles such as *Not Dead Yet* it is simply ignored.

Somehow I don't think Mark Latham had Reena, Allan, Netta or Andrea in mind when he wrote his essay. He hadn't had the benefit of hearing from those

26,000 members who have opened their lives, shared their fears and dreams, or understood the power inherent in their desires for a better future.

We need to build a Labor Party that provides pathways for workers like these to be heard and involved. Building these pathways will create challenges for unions and the party, but it is critical to rejuvenating Labor and ensuring it remains the champion for working people in this country. In turn, working people will have the chance to engage with and have confidence in the political process, asserting their right to have their voices heard and valued. You see, we're "not dead yet" either.

Louise Tarrant

Troy Bramston

Nine days after Gough Whitlam became leader of the Labor Party in 1967, the party's former leader, Arthur Calwell, addressed a trade union dinner in Sydney. "Those who wish to weaken the influence of the trade unions are enemies of the party and the trade union movement alike," he bellowed. "The Labor Party was founded by trade unions and nobody else. It has always been based on the trade union movement. It can never rest on any other foundation and still be the Labor Party." Sitting in the audience with a look of utter contempt on his face was the man who had replaced him as leader. Whitlam, however, was unfazed. He had filed an article for the next day's the *Australian* titled "Labor and the future." On the question of trade unions, Whitlam was clear. Labor's future as a party of the centre left with links to unions was not in doubt. But Labor's future role within the parliamentary system was at stake. "Our actions," he wrote, "in the next few years must determine whether [the party] continues to survive as a truly effective parliamentary force capable of governing and actually governing." Whitlam had fired the starting gun for the reform crusade that he would unleash as leader in the coming weeks. His mission was to dilute the power of the party's faction and union bosses, open up decision-making and rebuild the party's links with the community. He envisaged a Labor Party that was based not just on unions, but on the broad mass of people who represented modern Australia. More than four decades later, Labor is at the same reform crossroads.

Mark Latham's Quarterly Essay is a valuable addition to the growing debate about Labor's post-election challenges. There is, however, one area of vital reform on which he – and many others with good intentions, from John Faulkner and Darcy Byrne on the left to Sam Dastyari and Chris Bowen on the right – is silent: the party–union nexus. While Latham acknowledges the roots of "union power" in the party, its corrupting influence on policy and its corrosive impact on party culture, he does not offer any proposals for reform because he believes they will never succeed. As Latham told me when he was writing the essay, "I'm applying a discipline of looking for practical, feasible solutions." This is understandable. But this pragmatic approach has hemmed in one of the more astute observers among a class of Labor men and women who lack intellectual curiosity or a capacity to "dream the big dreams," as Paul Keating used to say. The holy grail of reform is to revisit the party's relationship with the trade union movement. Nothing is more fundamental to rebuilding the party's community links, renovating its policies or reforming its culture.

The recent Independent Commission against Corruption hearings into the former NSW Labor government have provided a window into the party–union relationship. The allegations of corruption levelled at the NSW Labor Right subfaction boss Eddie Obeid have been well aired. In April 2013, ICAC shifted its focus to the activities of the NSW Labor Left, which nurtured and supported the allegedly corrupt former minister Ian Macdonald. In February 2006, when the then NSW Labor assistant secretary Luke Foley told union bosses over a Chinese meal that he wanted to remove the faction's support for Macdonald to remain in the NSW upper house, he was overruled. Two powerful Left-aligned unions, the Construction, Forestry, Mining and Energy Union and the Australian Manufacturing Workers Union, would not wear it. Macdonald was endorsed for another term in the upper house, despite Foley's concerns. This is how power is exercised in the Labor Party.

To truly understand where power lies, it is necessary to examine the party's structural linkage with trade unions. Trade unions select 50 per cent of the delegates to the party's state conferences. Delegate numbers are allotted to a union based on that union's number of members. The delegation's composition is determined by the union secretary. At the conference, these delegates sit together and vote as one, as directed by the union secretary. This enables a union secretary to bargain with other powerbrokers to win their hoard of votes. Conferences decide on policy, elect party officials, and determine Senate and upper house pre-selections. Unions regard spots on the party's executive bodies as "theirs." They expect to have "their" delegates to the party's national conference elected by state conferences. They demand seats in parliament for "their" candidates. And they get them. This power is partly informal. Joel Fitzgibbon, the convenor of the NSW Labor Right in Canberra, told me in December 2012 that "trade union blocs" are able "to control individual MPs." Anybody in a position of power who challenges this – an MP, a party official, a conference delegate – will soon find their own position under threat. A faction, or faction boss, has power only because of the votes they control at party conferences. This is why reducing the proportion of union delegates to conferences is critical. Without a reduction from 50 per cent to perhaps 20 per cent, no reform will ever fundamentally transform who exercises power and how they exercise it. More broadly, the influence of unions throughout the party is pervasive. Most members of the government's front bench have either worked as a union representative or as a lawyer for unions. Unions send their staff to marginal seats to work on Labor campaigns. They pump money and other resources into local, state and national campaigns. At the coming federal election, unions affiliated to Labor are expected to draw on a war chest of around $5 million.

The hollowing-out of the party's membership – down from 150,000 in the 1930s to 50,000 in the 1990s, to 31,000 with two years' standing today – has been coupled with a rise in the influence of unions. As members have been squeezed out from participating in the party's key councils or standing as candidates for parliament, the influence of a political class dominated by unions and political staffers has grown inexorably. Concomitantly, the party in government has become vulnerable to policies that prop up old smokestack industries, re-regulate the labour market, denigrate skilled migration and spread ill-advised messages that propagate class warfare. The great party–union partnership for reform in the 1980s and 1990s has dissipated. As Bill Kelty argues, unions today lack leaders who are prepared to advocate trade-offs in return for economic reforms that are in the national interest. Whitlam, Bob Hawke and Keating were never beholden to unions to support their leadership. Kevin Rudd was, in part, undone by unions who witnessed his instinctive distrust of union power-brokers. Julia Gillard's leadership has been actively supported by trade union leaders who do not resile from their right to publicly state who should lead the party. Gillard has encouraged, even courted, an expansion of union power inside the government and the party. No leader since Calwell has been more beholden to, or more of an advocate for, trade union power.

The party was formed by the trade union movement in 1891. Born of the collective struggle for workers' rights, Labor has a sentimental link with unions as well as a structural one. In 1986 the NSW premier, Neville Wran, warned the party not to break its links with organised labour. But in 2011 he told me in an interview that Labor had "lost its way," as its candidates no longer represented the community. "On our side, it is university, union, ministerial or MP's office and then stand for an election," he said. "If you've been in that cloistered world, how can you expect to know what the real world is like?" Labor does not need to sever its links with unions, but it does need to reinvent them. Partly, it is about modernising the structure of the party to reflect the community. Whereas union density in the workforce was 40 per cent in 1990, today it is just 18 per cent, and falling. If unions no longer represent one-fifth of the workforce, how can they represent one-half of delegates to Labor conferences?

A few weeks after Whitlam became Labor leader, he addressed a Labour Day dinner in Melbourne. His speech was the polar opposite to Calwell's banquet oratory a few weeks earlier. Whitlam argued union participation in the party "must not merely be rhetorical, but real and representative of the whole trade union movement." Entrenching the power of union bosses, who propped up Calwell's leadership (as they do Gillard's today), was not what he had in mind. Whitlam wanted Labor once more to be a mass party that represented the vast cross-section of the community. Labor should consider how to encourage the 1 million affiliated union members – everyday men and women from a variety of trades and professions – to play a role inside the party, rather than be ruled by around 100 key union apparatchiks. Grassroots trade-union members could play a role in selecting local candidates, participating in policy development and perhaps helping to directly elect the party leader. But the critical structural link between unions and the party, cemented at state conferences with a 50 per cent bloc vote, should be reduced to around 20 per cent. Unless the party is prepared to slash the proportion of trade union delegates at its conferences, the vice-like grip that union and faction bosses have on Labor will never be broken.

Troy Bramston

	Correspondence

Nicholas Reece

One of the most powerful passages in Mark Latham's essay is when he writes of his own failure. For the first time I am aware of, he admits he came to the leadership too young at forty-two, with too little life experience and too much of his policy thinking still a work-in-progress. Latham's personal experience is surely a modern-day parable for the ALP. Now in his fifties, Latham is producing the most prescient work of his career. Yet at this very point he finds himself estranged from the party to which he gave twenty-five years of his life.

How did this happen?

Clearly Latham has a bit to answer for. His indiscretions and failings during his time as party leader have been extensively catalogued. But what has been less scrutinised is the role of the ALP in his ill-fated career trajectory. In less than two years the party catapulted Latham from relative obscurity to party leader, only to see him lose an election and then resign from parliament and quit the party. To go from obscurity to messiah to outcast in such a short period of time surely says as much about the organisation as it does about the individual.

Part of the explanation of this organisational shortcoming lies in the fact that political parties are strange beasts. The activities they undertake are important and complex, including electing MPs and leaders, formulating public policy and running campaigns. Yet their corporate culture is very different to that of other enterprises undertaking similar activities, such as the public service, academic institutions or even advertising firms. Instead, as the academic Glyn Davis and others have detailed, political parties and their parliamentary groupings have an ethos which is more akin to that of a street gang, those groups of disenfranchised youths who band together for mutual profit and support.

Latham is a case in point. In a different organisation he would have been recognised as a promising talent who needed more time in middle management before he was ready for a leadership role. Instead, the desperate gang, in this case the federal Labor caucus, decided he fit the bill and made him their leader. For a short while he was hailed as a new messiah. But then fortunes changed, the tenuous bargain between the leader and the gang unravelled and Latham was brutally cast out. He retired from politics at just forty-three, with his best years still a decade away. While much has been made of Labor's revolving door of party leadership, the Liberal Party is just as susceptible to this ruthless and unforgiving modus operandi – after all, it has had four leaders in just over five years.

The situation is made possible by a parliamentary system in which the leader holds office with the consent of the party room, which is made up of MPs from the same party. In this way, in a nation of 23 million people, a person can be elected the leader of the Labor or Liberal party, and even prime minister, with the votes of between just thirty-five and fifty-five of their party colleagues.

Given Latham's searing personal experience, there is one party reform proposal that I am surprised he did not advocate. That reform is the direct election of the party leader by the rank-and-file members of the party. If such a model was in place, it is unlikely that Latham would have been elected leader when he was. Instead he would have needed a few more years to build his profile. It is also possible that his departure would not have been so swift.

Over the last two decades progressive and conservative political parties around the world have introduced institutional reforms that give ordinary party members a direct vote in the election of the party leader. In the United Kingdom and Canada, which are Westminster parliamentary democracies like Australia, all the major parties now give rank-and-file members a say in choosing the leader. These changes mean these democracies do not have the revolving door of party leadership that is a feature of politics Down Under, nor do they suffer from the mindless media-driven leadership speculation that we must endure. Moreover, their political parties have membership figures the Australian parties can only dream of.

Latham details the decline in membership of the ALP, likening the modern party to a Hollywood back lot with nothing behind the façade. The ALP has a national membership of around 40,000. The Liberal Party is in a similar situation. The major Australian political parties now have fewer members than many AFL football clubs and struggle to staff voting booths properly on election day.

Direct election of the leader by party members could help reverse this decline. One of the many similarities that Australia and Canada used to share was the fact that we had close to the lowest level of political-party membership of any Western democracy. But as result of party reforms in Canada it is now Australia that holds the wooden spoon for citizen engagement with political parties. Last year Canada's left-of-centre, trade union–supported New Democratic Party held a ballot of its members for the leadership. As part of the election campaign, the party signed up 45,000 new people and now has 130,000 members. The other major progressive political party in Canada is the Liberal Party. It registered 130,000 members and supporters to participate in a leadership ballot in April 2013. Meanwhile the Conservative Party used a similar model to elect Steven Harper as its leader in 2004, with a ballot of its 100,000 members.

Sooner or later the Australian political parties are going to work out how unusual they have become by international standards. The crisis in membership numbers together with the problems caused by the rapid turnover of leaders makes it inevitable that one of the major parties will move to give ordinary members a direct vote for the leader. And once one major party makes the change, the other will doubtless follow.

Latham's main proposal for party reform involves the introduction of community-based primary pre-selections that allow party members and registered "supporters" to vote for the local candidate. He argues that local primaries will attract new branch members and volunteers, pre-select better candidates, provide a valuable profile boost for the successful candidate for the election and transform the party's culture through community engagement.

As Secretary of the ALP in Victoria I was involved in Australia's first primary pre-selection, held in the outer metropolitan state seat of Kilsyth in 2010. The Kilsyth primary and subsequent primaries held in some NSW seats have enjoyed modest success. The accusation that primaries will give rise to "money politics and corruption" has not been evident in the trials to date. Opposition to primaries comes from vested interests in the ALP who see them as a challenge to their power base. It also comes from those in the rank and file who see primaries as devaluing their own party membership by allowing "non-members" to vote in party elections. Nonetheless, community-based primaries have had enough success to warrant their further trial, including in a winnable parliamentary seat.

The bigger point to be made here is that the ALP needs to do something. The party of reform needs to show it is able to reform itself. The party founded on a radical democratic experiment needs to show it is still capable of democratic innovation. It cannot keep commissioning major reviews by party elders and then ignore the more challenging findings. A bit of experimentation and trial and error should be embraced. The federal structure of the party is useful in this regard: mistakes can be confined to a single state, while success can be rolled out nationally.

A reform package aimed at increasing member support could involve a further trial of primaries in some winnable seats, together with direct election of the party leader by ordinary members. This injection of democracy at the top and bottom of the party would present a grand bargain to party members: on the one hand, they give up some of the power of their membership by giving "supporters" a vote in local elections, but on the other, they get a new power to cast a vote for the party leader. Together these reforms build a bigger and stronger party that stands more chance of electoral success.

In writing this piece I am conscious that I have added further pages to the national pastime of speculating on the future of the ALP. Much of this work is not helpful. So I finish by noting that none of this should be seriously debated this side of the September federal election.

The single best thing the ALP could do for itself is to win an election. A victory in a significant state or federal election would help bring some perspective back to the forecasts of demise for Australia's oldest and largest progressive political party. After all, it was just over four years ago that the ALP held government nationally and in every state and territory in Australia.

Nicholas Reece

Mark Latham

Thank you to each of the reviewers for their time and thoughtfulness in reading the essay and then writing about it. I studied each contribution at length before deciding how to focus this rejoinder. I apologise to Peter Brent and Guy Rundle for not being able to make specific remarks in response to their well-written reviews.

Elsewhere, I must confess, I found Russell Marks's assessment that "Latham's analysis of modern Labor is all wrong" somewhat discouraging. Couldn't I just be partly wrong, instead of wasting each and every one of my 25,000 words? A few sentences later, however, I took new heart, as Marks argued, "the party now lacks a workable theory of power which would allow it to take on vested economic interests in the name of the common good."

In fact, Not Dead Yet sets out a theory of power which has worked in practice: the Keating model of economic openness, placing a heavy competitive discipline on capitalists, while generating productivity and income benefits for wage-earners. A generation of working-class families has benefited from Australia's Labor-inspired economic miracle. The Keating model positions Labor as pro-market but not necessarily pro-business (as defined by caving into corporate demands for protection, subsidies and other forms of business welfare).

In any case, the essay was not aimed at Marks and other devotees of class struggle. Given my standing as what one correspondent described as a "fading gurgle of political failure," I wanted to pass on a few lessons to Labor's next generation before I disappear entirely down the plughole of public life. Thus I am greatly encouraged by the responses of Nicholas Reece, Andrew Charlton, Troy Bramston and Jim Chalmers. If Labor is to have a future, it is in their hands.

Reece has picked up an important point: as the pace of modern politics has grown faster, the career steps of Labor's young hopefuls need to proceed at a slower rate. If nothing else, I am a living monument to the problem of crash-and-burn. So too, I have no doubt, Kevin Rudd and Julia Gillard would have enjoyed more successful prime ministerships if they had taken on the Labor leadership in their late fifties, instead of their late forties.

When under siege from the relentless whinging of the Murdoch media, talk-back radio and Australia's *Fox News* equivalent at Sky, maturity – and with it, a rollicking sense of life's absurdities – is a Labor leader's greatest asset. Eventually, they come for all of us, so preparation is all-important. Old Jack Lang used to tell young Laborites that they didn't have a moment to spare in advancing their prospects. Now the opposite is true. Every step needs to be a well-planned and patient one.

Charlton has provided an insightful summary of my intellectual journey, while Bramston has drilled into Labor's contentious organisational links with the union movement – a problem brewing since the time of Whitlam. Both have the party's best interests in mind. But my greatest debt is to Chalmers for making me rethink the idea of insiders and outsiders.

I first spoke about this framework ten years ago as a way of conceiving the new political divide – or, as Jim calls it, "the fragmentation of constituencies." I identified elites to the far-right and far-left of Labor, privileged insiders who dealt with issues in a manner abstracted from the practical realities of suburban life. The ALP, in my argument, needed to position itself as a party dispersing economic, social and political influence. It needed to empower the outsiders – our logical support base. Importantly, the dispersal process involved the redistribution of public resources to areas of greatest need.

This schema had the virtue of rhetorical appeal, rallying the party to a new push against inequality. In practice, however, it underestimated the importance of two factors. The first was the political risk of redistribution in an increasingly aspirational electorate. Within Labor's culture, we call taking from the privileged and giving to the less-privileged "fairness" – a basic definition. But now, for many suburban families, they judge their social standing not by their current position but by their (expected) future status. Thus redistributive policies threaten their expectations in life.

Under John Howard and now Tony Abbott, the conservatives (in parliament and the media) have worked out a strategy for exploiting this sentiment. They demonise redistribution as "class warfare," as if Labor is refighting the Russian Revolution. This is how the Tories responded to our relatively modest proposal in 2004 for the reallocation of school funding (the so-called hit-list – a term still used today by politicians and commentators whose children attend elite private schools). More recently, the tactic was also deployed in the mining-tax controversy. Another modest redistributive Labor policy was portrayed as a threat to national prosperity and the aspirations of future mining entrepreneurs.

The second factor I underestimated was the impact of Australia's long economic boom on the outsiders themselves. With the rise of a more self-reliant citizenry, a declining number of people actually see themselves as outsiders. The near-universal increase in disposable incomes over the past twenty-five years has given a significant number of households the power to buy in private education, health and recreation services. The rise of mass education, such that 57 per cent of Australian adults now hold post-secondary qualifications, has fostered greater skills and self-confidence across the population. In the information age, people have never been better informed (on subjects that interest them) or more articulate. Other than in heavily disadvantaged communities, feelings of powerlessness have dissipated.

It was only after I left parliament that I began to fully understand this change. MPs are trapped in a culture which emphasises problems in society. Nobody comes to electorate offices to talk about their new job and new-found affluence. They come only with problems. So too, the commercial media specialises in a doomsday view of the world. Outside this political bubble, Australia is a very different place. The social impact of rising prosperity and self-reliance has been phenomenal.

The nature of political power is changing, but not as I expected. Moisés Naim's book offers a more reliable guide. The old institutions of democracy have hollowed out – concentrating influence in the hands of those who still participate in political parties and movements – while elsewhere in society, people have become more self-sufficient. Voters have less need for government and less interest in party politics. This has produced a cross-currents effect: the concentration of residual power inside parties versus the dispersal of social and economic influence outside politics. A decade ago, as I was issuing a clarion call to empower the outsiders, the work was already being done by the Hawke–Keating economic revolution.

Increasingly, those involved in the two-party system are rusted-on partisans. Labor has fallen back on its core trade-union base, while the Liberal Party is now dominated by right-wing fanatics: Tea Party-style ideologues, the Religious Right and the growing presence of authoritarian figures from a Northern European background. Publicly, the full impact of this change will not be apparent until such time as the conservatives regain office in Canberra.

Organisationally, the task for Labor is self-evident: to broaden its base through community pre-selections for all seats in all houses, in all parliaments. What does the party have to fear from giving local people a vote? The representative nature of Labor caucuses needs to be enhanced by bringing creative entrepreneurs, service sector workers and tradies into parliament, to join a (diminished) core of trade union officials and factional heavies. If, as the polls suggest, the Gillard government is defeated in September, the first twelve months in opposition should be spent on major organisational change. Logic requires it, and the electorate expects it. The stain of factional arrogance which generated the HSU scandal and ICAC inquiries in New South Wales must be removed.

In policy, a turning point has been reached. In an electorate with a high degree of self-reliance, there is less work for social democrats to do. The assumptions of Whitlamism about service delivery – so enabling and enlightening in their time – are not as relevant. The great breakthrough in Whitlam's thinking in the 1960s was that the needs and aspirations of suburban Australia could only be satisfied by a bigger role for government. He ended the party's narrow focus on nationalisation and industrial relations by developing a new agenda for education, health and urban services. The best summary of this vision was in Gough's 1969 policy speech:

> We of the Labor Party have an enduring commitment to a view about society. It is this: in modern countries, opportunities for all citizens – the opportunity for a complete education, opportunity for dignity in retirement, opportunity for proper medical treatment, opportunity to share in the nation's wealth and resources, opportunity for decent housing, the opportunity for civilised conditions in our cities and our towns, opportunity to preserve and promote the natural beauty of the land – can be provided only if governments – the community itself acting through its elected representatives – will provide them. Private wealth is insufficient now to provide such opportunities even for the wealthy few. The inequalities in our community now reflect not so much gross disparities in income, but the failure of successive Liberal governments to create opportunities for the overwhelming majority of our people – the lower, modest and middle income families – opportunities which only governments can make.

For four decades, following the election of the Whitlam government, Labor has been on a long march of state-led service delivery. The Hawke and Keating governments honoured the Whitlam legacy through Medicare, national super-annuation, mass university education and environmental protection. Rudd and Gillard have moved forward with DisabilityCare, Gonski school funding, paid parental leave, public housing reform and the NBN. Each of the markers of a modern, civilised, cradle-to-grave welfare state is now in place. The great man can rest easy. His work is done.

What, then, is the task for the next generation of Laborites? Obviously, to pre-serve the gains of social democratic reform: the Keating economic model and Whitlamite service delivery. But also to recognise a new reality: many Australians can buy in services for themselves. Twenty years of economic boom have given families a purchasing power of which their parents and grandparents could only dream. Today, for most citizens and communities, the private sector is no less capable of meeting their needs than the public sector. Equilibrium has been reached in the age-old ideological struggle between individuals and the state.

The long debate about the appropriate role of government is over. And Labor has won. The party has governed nationally for twenty-one of the past forty years and successfully implemented a great social and economic reform pro-gram. There is much to celebrate, in a legacy worth protecting, but also a basic truth to confront. There is little need to expand further the responsibilities of government. Vigilance will be required as the Tea Party boys try to roll back Labor's gains, but through internal debate, in the framework of Labor policy, the issue is essentially settled.

The party should now think about its role in terms of "light-touch social democracy." Future Labor governments will not need to be a whirring frenzy of activity, with senior ministers trying to micromanage scores of issues simul-taneously. Rather, with responsible economic policies and government's social democratic core intact, they can focus on three priorities:

- The importance of education policy through all stages of life (what we used to call "lifelong learning") – in particular, schools reform and expanding access to post-secondary qualifications.
- The alleviation of poverty and the underclass, ensuring all Australians can enjoy the benefits of self-reliance.
- The looming climate change disruption, positioning Labor as the party best suited to mediating economic and environmental tensions later this century.

This light-touch approach makes sense in terms of the party's achievements. In all probability, it will also be an electoral necessity. For the next decade or so,

Labor leaders will need to work overtime in rebuilding the party's reputation for sound fiscal management – a rerun of Bill Hayden's task after 1977. After two decades of sustained economic growth, the federal budget should be in surplus. The best way of restoring this fiscal discipline is to pare back the scale of social democratic ambition.

This is not an invitation for quietism or policy inertia, but rather a question of balance: consolidating past gains while understanding that the good society now relies on a more targeted approach to public sector growth. Reformers no longer need to be here, there and everywhere, Kevin-style. Rudd was a highly skilled media performer, but as a government leader he had little sense of priorities. In trying to be all things to all people he ended up as nothing to anyone, especially his colleagues (who saw the administrative chaos first-hand).

The post-war welfare state does not require a rolling program of reinvention. Rather, it needs selective improvement. Given the intensity and high attrition rate of modern politics, Labor MPs are likely to benefit from ring-fencing the scope of reform – working on fewer projects with greater effectiveness. It might actually be time for a cup of tea and an Iced VoVo.

A light touch would also assist in avoiding the pitfalls of redistributive policy. Labor's goal should be to lift up from the bottom, not to knock down from the top. Wise heads need to overrule old hatreds. I love nothing better in life than giving it to toffee-nosed, North Shore spivs, but the political utility of this approach has expired. I'm an anti-model for how to handle the elites. In any case, the lessons of the Rudd and Gillard governments have made the point clearly. Contrast the political impact and feasibility of the Gonski funding reforms (lifting up from the bottom) with the mining resource rent tax (knocking down from the top). Gonski is a good model for how to minimise interest-group resistance to new social justice strategies.

*

In her review, Louise Tarrant from United Voice tries to portray me as an out-of-touch member of the "commentariat" – someone who knows nothing about workers in the child care, aged care, cleaning, security and hospitality sectors. Far from recently dropping into this debate, I know many hundreds of people from a working-class background. I grew up with them. I went to school with them. I represented them for seventeen years in local and federal government.

I still see them, socialising with them, in my local community in Sydney's south-west. I serve with them on the P & Cs of the government schools my children attend. Just last week, I was a referee for a friend who has worked in child care for ten years and now hopes to get a new (and better) job at an aged-care facility in Liverpool.

When I left parliament I could have easily moved to Sydney's North Shore, to the eastern suburbs or the inner-city – a common pattern among former Labor MPs, even trade union officials. But I stayed in the region where I grew up, the place where I feel I belong. Watching the changes in Western Sydney over the past thirty years has taught me to appreciate the success of the Keating economic model. When NATSEM reported a 27 per cent increase in real disposable incomes for the poorest 20 per cent of Australian households since the mid-1980s, I found it thoroughly believable.

This is one of the interesting features of Australia's "doomsday coalition" – activists like Tarrant on the left (who wish the Keating model had never been implemented) and a galaxy of Tea Party-style whingers on the right. They never quote national economic statistics. They never cite figures for growth in GDP, employment, national income and productivity. Instead, they rely on populist horror stories, cameos of families supposedly having "to sweat, freeze or live in darkness because [they] can't afford power."

With Australia's decent minimum wage, strong jobs market and generous family payments system, no child-care worker, hotel receptionist, school cleaner or security guard need turn off their power box, other than for reasons of household budget waste and mismanagement. I asked my job-seeking friend about this scenario and she replied: "I would rather see electricity prices going down than up, but can we still afford air-conditioning and lighting? Yeah sure, no problem."

If the Keating model had created mass unemployment and cut living standards in seats like Werriwa, Fowler and Macarthur, I would not have supported it. But the opposite is true. It has liberated hundreds of thousands of families from low-skill, repetitive factory work and given their children and grandchildren a crack at professional jobs and business ownership. I don't want to be too cranky about this, but I don't need Tarrant to lecture me on the people I know and the things I see every day.

As for listening to cleaners, I have been doing it for as long as I can remember. My mother was a school cleaner. Before that she worked in a box factory. She had little personal ambition in life other than fostering a capacity for hard work and educational striving in her children and grandchildren. Through the power of government schools and universities, her grandchildren now include a medical specialist, trainee GP, computer programming expert and television ratings statistician, plus a budding author, movie director and newspaper editor (a genetic flaw somewhere in the family). This is the real world in which I live.

It is indicative of the pace of social mobility in the new economy. The success of the Whitlam, Hawke, Keating, Rudd and Gillard governments in broadening educational access has produced a tremendous amount of socio-economic churning, most of it upwards. We are now a far more egalitarian country than during the Menzies era, when only three out of every 100 working-age Australians had higher education qualifications. Most children grew up expecting to work in occupations little different to their parents. Labor has lifted the university attainment rate to twenty-five out of every 100, with a goal of reaching 40 per cent by 2020.

Last year the OECD reported on comparative rates of educational mobility in member nations. Australia ranked tenth out of twenty-seven countries – an encouraging performance, especially given the deadweight funding cuts of the Fraser and Howard years. The odds of someone whose parents have low levels of educational attainment reaching university in Australia are 47 per cent. This compares favourably with other English-speaking nations, such as New Zealand (21 per cent), Canada (22) and the United States (29). We even ranked ahead of two Scandinavian countries: Norway (39) and Finland (43), plus most of continental Europe.

In 2011, NATSEM and the Smith Family reported on intergenerational mobility in education. They compared the qualifications of people born between 1964 and 1978 with those of their fathers (at a time when the children were fourteen years of age). This was a large cohort, but not one which had fully realised the benefits of post-secondary expansion under the Hawke–Keating and Rudd–Gillard governments. Nonetheless, the cross-currents of intergenerational mobility point to substantially improved social fairness.

For the children of fathers with a tertiary qualification, 34.1 per cent failed to replicate their paternal heritage by going to university. More than 20 per cent did not get past "Year 12 or Below." Among the children of fathers who got no further than years 11 and 12, 53.4 per cent went to university. For families in which the father had a vocational qualification, this figure was 41.5 per cent. For the children of relatively uneducated fathers ("Year 10 or Below"), 29.3 per cent achieved a university degree. While these figures are not perfect, they highlight the capacity of educational access to break down entrenched centres of disadvantage and privilege.

This should be a foundation stone for Labor's future. The party should now aim at 85 per cent post-secondary attainment. Mass education links Labor's economic agenda with its social justice goals. It bridges a wide range of constituencies:

inner-city progressives, suburban aspirationals and underclass communities; insiders and outsiders. It's also crucial in the evolution of progressive social values.

Education gives people a broader understanding of the society in which they live, fostering the habits of tolerance and respect for difference across racial and cultural boundaries. It encourages people to appreciate the circumstances of the less privileged, using reason instead of prejudice. Studies have shown how educational attainment correlates positively with support for social justice and collective solutions to problems.

This is why Tories hate it. Recently, I engaged in a few "culture war" skirmishes with one of News Limited's ideological spear-carriers, Nick Cater, following the release of his book *The Lucky Culture*. A striking feature of his thesis is the way in which it attacks higher education for fostering progressive beliefs. His solution is to wind back university access in Australia to the standard set by Keith Murray in his report to the Menzies government in 1957. As Cater explains it, only "16 per cent of the Australian population had the intellectual ability to succeed at university" – a sifting process he supports for today's system. In practice, this means expelling one-third of the student population (reducing university attainment from 25 per cent back to 16). Abbott has endorsed *The Lucky Culture* as a "perceptive book" and "shrewd analysis."

When the Liberals talk about ending "the age of entitlement," they are not referring to middle-class welfare. During the Howard years, they created more new middle-class welfare entitlements than any other government in Australian history. Abbott is already heading in this direction, preserving a $4.5 billion annual entitlement for carbon tax compensation, even though he plans to abolish the tax. This is the Liberal equivalent of bad-back syndrome: compo for nothing. When the Tea Party attacks come, they will be against "culture war" targets, most notably universities and the ABC. If Labor loses in September, tertiary education access will be a key battleline.

*

Tarrant could not be more mistaken when she writes: "Somehow I don't think Mark Latham had Reena, Allan, Netta or Andrea in mind when he wrote his essay." If they are anything like my mother and other parents I know in Western Sydney, they too will see education as an essential pathway for their children. When I write about reforms to give Australia a high-performing government-school system, I have in mind the realisation of the greatest of working-class dreams: success in life for the next generation. I regard United Voice members as part of Australia's aspirational class. They have no less ambition for their family than higher income earners. So too, when I write about the benefits of the Keating model in generating new jobs and higher disposable incomes, I'm not thinking of Gina Rinehart or James Packer. I have in mind folk like Reena, Allan, Netta and Andrea.

Tarrant has misunderstood the argument in *Not Dead Yet*. I haven't said lower income working families have disappeared entirely or industrial safeguards – including the vital work of trade unions – should be abolished. There will always be a role for industrial labour recruiting members and organising in workplaces. But it is, as a proportion of the workforce, a diminished role. And by necessity, it must be a diminished influence inside the party.

If Tarrant believes this is a viable political base for Labor's future, she needs to get in quick. I love the working class, its values, its sincerity, its irreverent outlook on life. In many ways, it breaks my heart to see Australia losing these things. If the role of Labor is to lock people into a fixed socio-economic standing – ensuring a stable membership base for Tarrant's union – then the Keating economic experiment has failed. If, however, the party's role is to ensure Reena's, Allan's, Netta's and Andrea's children can work in better jobs and earn higher incomes than their parents, then Labor in government has done wonderful things. As they say out my way: "What's the difference between a working-class family and middle-class family in Western Sydney? One generation."

Finally, Tarrant writes that I have advocated "a complete fracturing of the relationship between the party and unions." In fact, the Quarterly Essay recognises the permanence of Labor's union links. It advocates a change in organisational direction through the introduction of community pre-selections. I am surprised Tarrant sees this as a "fracturing of the relationship." The proposal is to give Reena, Allan, Netta and Andrea a voice in the selection of Labor candidates. For the first time, all United Voice members, if they choose to participate in their federal and state electorates, would have a say as to who the party puts forward at election time. By getting rank-and-file unionists directly involved in party decision-making, the relationship between unions and local ALP branches can be enhanced.

The only fracturing that community pre-selections are likely to cause is in the power of union secretaries, such as Tarrant. Within Labor's current tight-knit factional system, her union has a big voice in the selection of Labor candidates, especially for upper house seats. Why can't Reena, Allan, Netta and Andrea also have a say? Real Voices for Change sounds like a fine union initiative. Why can't its principles be applied to broadening Labor's base and relevance at a community level?

I have no doubt Tarrant is a well-intended person who cares deeply about the welfare of her members. I would ask her, however, to understand how political parties run the risk of dying when their traditional base evaporates. Without the creation of new constituencies, it can be a long and fractious death. Her union will survive, but the ALP might not.

This is what I find worrying about her response. Tarrant wants to limit Labor's core function to protecting the workplace conditions of a shrinking proportion of the electorate, while preserving the party's union/factional hier-archy. This may well be the direction the party takes. Perhaps I have been too optimistic in thinking other options are viable. If so, union officials like Tarrant should have no doubt or confusion as to what it means politically. It turns the ALP into just another interest group, a fringe party pitching its policies and message at 10 to 15 per cent of the electorate. Dead yet? Under this scenario, almost certainly so.

Mark Latham

Troy Bramston is a columnist with the *Australian*. He is the author of *Looking for the Light on the Hill: Modern Labor's Challenges* and editor of *For the True Believers: Great Labor Speeches That Shaped History*. His next book, *The Whitlam Legacy*, will be published later this year.

Peter Brent has a PhD in political science and has been writing about politics since 2001 on his blog *Mumble*, which is now hosted by the *Australian*.

Jim Chalmers is executive director of the Chifley Research Centre, following long stints as chief of staff to the deputy prime minister and treasurer, senior adviser to state and federal Labor leaders, and national research manager for the Australian Labor Party. He has a PhD in political science and an honours degree in public policy. His first book, *Glory Daze*, will be published in 2013.

Andrew Charlton was senior economic adviser to Prime Minister Kevin Rudd from 2008 to 2010. He received his doctorate in economics from Oxford University, where he studied as a Rhodes Scholar, and is the author of Quarterly Essay 44, *Man-Made World: Choosing between Progress and Planet*, *Ozonomics* and *Fair Trade for All*, co-written with Nobel laureate Joseph Stiglitz.

Anna Goldsworthy is the author of *Piano Lessons* and *Welcome To Your New Life*. Her writing has appeared in the *Monthly*, the *Age*, the *Australian*, the *Adelaide Review* and *Best Australian Essays*. She is also a concert pianist, with several recordings to her name.

Mark Latham was leader of the Australian Labor Party and leader of the Opposition from December 2003 to January 2005. His books include *Civilising Global Capital* and the bestselling *Latham Diaries*. He has a column in the *Australian Financial Review*.

Russell Marks is a Melbourne-based lawyer and former university lecturer. He has compiled two books of quotations for Black Inc., *Tony Speaks: The Wisdom of the Abbott* and *Kattertonia: The Wit and Wisdom of Bob Katter*, and is working on a biography of a well-known public intellectual.

Nicholas Reece has worked as the Victorian ALP secretary and a senior adviser to Prime Minister Julia Gillard and to former Victorian state premiers Steve Bracks and John Brumby. He is now a fellow at the University of Melbourne's Centre for Public Policy.

Guy Rundle is a writer-at-large for *Crikey* and the author of Quarterly Essay 3, *The Opportunist: John Howard and the Triumph of Reaction*. His most recent book is the award-winning *Down to the Crossroads: On the Trail of the 2008 US Election*.

Louise Tarrant is a lifelong unionist who is currently the national secretary of United Voice, one of Australia's largest unions.

SUBSCRIBE to Quarterly Essay & SAVE over 25% on the cover price

Subscriptions: Receive a discount and never miss an issue. Mailed direct to your door.

☐ **1 year subscription** (4 issues): $59 within Australia incl. GST. Outside Australia $89.

☐ **2 year subscription** (8 issues): $105 within Australia incl. GST. Outside Australia $165.

* All prices include postage and handling.

Back Issues: (Prices include postage and handling.)

☐ **QE 2** ($15.95) John Birmingham *Appeasing Jakarta*
☐ **QE 4** ($15.95) Don Watson *Rabbit Syndrome*
☐ **QE 6** ($15.95) John Button *Beyond Belief*
☐ **QE 7** ($15.95) John Martinkus *Paradise Betrayed*
☐ **QE 8** ($15.95) Amanda Lohrey *Groundswell*
☐ **QE 10** ($15.95) Gideon Haigh *Bad Company*
☐ **QE 11** ($15.95) Germaine Greer *Whitefella Jump Up*
☐ **QE 12** ($15.95) David Malouf *Made in England*
☐ **QE 13** ($15.95) Robert Manne with David Corlett *Sending Them Home*
☐ **QE 14** ($15.95) Paul McGeough *Mission Impossible*
☐ **QE 15** ($15.95) Margaret Simons *Latham's World*
☐ **QE 17** ($15.95) John Hirst *"Kangaroo Court"*
☐ **QE 18** ($15.95) Gail Bell *The Worried Well*
☐ **QE 19** ($15.95) Judith Brett *Relaxed & Comfortable*
☐ **QE 20** ($15.95) John Birmingham *A Time for War*
☐ **QE 21** ($15.95) Clive Hamilton *What's Left?*
☐ **QE 22** ($15.95) Amanda Lohrey *Voting for Jesus*
☐ **QE 23** ($15.95) Inga Clendinnen *The History Question*
☐ **QE 24** ($15.95) Robyn Davidson *No Fixed Address*
☐ **QE 25** ($15.95) Peter Hartcher *Bipolar Nation*

☐ **QE 26** ($15.95) David Marr *His Master's Voice*
☐ **QE 27** ($15.95) Ian Lowe *Reaction Time*
☐ **QE 28** ($15.95) Judith Brett *Exit Right*
☐ **QE 29** ($15.95) Anne Manne *Love & Money*
☐ **QE 30** ($15.95) Paul Toohey *Last Drinks*
☐ **QE 31** ($15.95) Tim Flannery *Now or Never*
☐ **QE 32** ($15.95) Kate Jennings *American Revolution*
☐ **QE 33** ($15.95) Guy Pearse *Quarry Vision*
☐ **QE 34** ($15.95) Annabel Crabb *Stop at Nothing*
☐ **QE 36** ($15.95) Mungo MacCallum *Australian Story*
☐ **QE 37** ($15.95) Waleed Aly *What's Right?*
☐ **QE 38** ($15.95) David Marr *Power Trip*
☐ **QE 39** ($15.95) Hugh White *Power Shift*
☐ **QE 42** ($15.95) Judith Brett *Fair Share*
☐ **QE 43** ($15.95) Robert Manne *Bad News*
☐ **QE 44** ($15.95) Andrew Charlton *Man-Made World*
☐ **QE 45** ($15.95) Anna Krien *Us and Them*
☐ **QE 46** ($15.95) Laura Tingle *Great Expectations*
☐ **QE 47** ($15.95) David Marr *Political Animal*
☐ **QE 48** ($15.95) Tim Flannery *After the Future*
☐ **QE 49** ($15.95) Mark Latham *Not Dead Yet*

Payment Details: I enclose a cheque/money order made out to Schwartz Media Pty Ltd. Please debit my credit card (Mastercard or Visa accepted).

Card No. ☐ ☐ ☐ ☐ ☐ ☐ ☐ ☐ ☐ ☐ ☐ ☐ ☐ ☐ ☐ ☐

Expiry date ___ / ___   **CCV** ___   **Amount $** _____

Cardholder's name _____   **Signature** _____

Name _____

Address _____

Email _____   **Phone** _____

Post or fax this form to: Quarterly Essay, Reply Paid 79448, Collingwood VIC 3066 / Tel: (03) 9486 0288 / Fax: (03) 9486 0244 / Email: subscribe@blackincbooks.com Subscribe online at **www.quarterlyessay.com**